What the Industry is Saying –

MW00570987

"I've had the pleasure of working with _____ years and know firsthand how his ap _____ unparalleled. Darren leaves not a sing _____ the event to feel liquid, organic, and fun! Darren was able to outline how he approaches events in a really fun and informative way and if you do what he says–the way he says it–your event will be a great success, and just as important, fun and memorable for those involved. Darren's tips are priceless for a great event. Good luck, and have fun!"

> Bob Guiney
> TV host and Bachelor Bob from ABC's hit
> TV show *The Bachelor*

"For anyone wanting to be in the event business, this is a must-read book that highlights the importance of communication, strategy, and how to think on your feet, especially when 'stuff happens' in the exciting but not-so-perfect world of corporate event planning. This book should be mandatory reading for industry students and professionals alike. Darren's entertaining real-world stories will help anyone in most situations, as well as provide a laugh or two. This book will help you know if this business is for you and how to succeed once you're in it."

> Bill Quain, Ph.D.
> Author/Professor
> Formerly–University of Nevada Las Vegas

"As an instructor at a four-year university teaching within the event management curriculum, I found Darren's book a fast, easy read. Real world examples of the corporate planning industry will capture my students' undivided attention. Darren's tips are so spot-on and I plan to share them with my students and others looking to get into this industry!"

> Premila Whitney, Instructor
> University of Central Florida
> Hospitality Management

"If you are organizing any type of event (small or large), read, absorb, and use the brilliant strategies in this amazing book by Darren Johnson. There is a reason he is hired to produce events and consults for the biggest companies in America–because Darren is the BEST!"

> James Malinchak
> Featured on ABC's hit TV show
> *Secret Millionaire*

"The attention to detail and helpful hints to planning an event are clearly represented in the book. These suggestions and recommendations will be helpful to anyone wanting to accomplish success in the world of events and event planning."

> Michael Gozik
> Orlando Theme Park Resorts

"Darren Johnson crafts events for demanding clients in real-world conditions. He seems to know in his soul what guests crave for a good time. While others serve up trendy and flashy events trying to be unique with no regard for what works in the trenches, Darren is a southern Peter Pan of a party boy who believes we all deserve a good time and he is just the guy to create the fun!"

John J. Ekin IV
Professional international cruise ship entertainer
and former White House entertainer

"For anyone starting out in the event planning business, this book will give you insider information that would take you years to learn on your own… usually the hard way! For industry veterans, it can be a great refresher on information you may have long forgotten, and I'll bet in many cases a prep course on scenarios you may have never encountered. Either way, you will come away better prepared for your next big event."

Lee Peyton
Peyton Entertainment Productions

"Darren's book is an easy-to-read planning tool for anyone producing any kind of event from a personal wedding to a large-scale corporate production. His tips and stories make the book fun and informational while providing must-have organizational and scheduling ideas."

Jill Swidler
Director of Marketing
Legoland

"I have known and worked with Darren for many years. In fact, my destination management company used Darren exclusively for all of its event and production needs. He never lets us down. Darren really knows his stuff! This book provides a wealth of valuable information and quickly demonstrates the depth of Darren's knowledge and experience."

Fritz Lehman
Founder, Hello Florida Destination
Management Company

"Darren Johnson knows his STUFF! Combining his extensive knowledge of corporate event planning and his sense of humor (which you MUST have in this business!) Darren has written a book that is packed with valuable information and provides ideas and suggestions that are tried and true! Darren's book covers all the angles–from the little details to the big picture to make sure events come off without a hitch! I am proud to say that I have had the pleasure of working with Darren on various projects, and they were very successful."

Susan Robinson, CMP
Vice President, Incentives and Corporate Travel
Stifel Nicolaus

"Great reading, great ideas, great tips! Darren was able to put his 30 years of experience into print. This book is filled with useful information, strategies, and industry secrets that an education and classroom cannot teach you."

David Ball
Director of Convention Center Operations
Caribe Royale Orlando

"If you are looking for a proven approach to really connecting with your audience through a corporate event, Darren Johnson's latest book, *Going Live: Insider Secrets To Corporate Event Production* is a lifesaver. This is the premier book on event production, revealing not only the art but the science of how to implement with a time-tested roadmap."

John Michel, Senior Director
ITAGroup Inc., a leading corporate travel company

"As an Emmy-award-winning–director and producer, I know what it takes to pull off a 'show', but man, the stuff Darren pulls off live is on a whole different level! I absolutely agree with the strategies, principles, and practices that Darren outlines in *Going Live: Insider Secrets to Corporate Event Production*. It is a must-read for every student and professional involved in live event production."

Nick Nanton, CEO
The Celebrity Branding Agency

"As a former corporate executive for more than 20 years for a multibillion-dollar publicly traded company, I understand the importance of effective, results-oriented corporate event producers. Their success is ultimately my success. Darren's strategies and techniques will contribute to your success."

Dave Tyburski
Chief Profit Officer
James Malinchak International, Inc.

"From beginning to end, *Going Live* provides vivid, real-life perspective and a true insider's view of the roller-coaster ride that is event planning. Darren's insight will be enthusiastically welcomed by rookie and veteran planners alike. His essential elements cover the spectrum from planning strategy to tactical delivery and translate seamlessly from the pages to practical actions. That will help you as a professional and make your program exceed expectations."

Michael A. Willis, Manager
Field Sales and Broker Loyalty
Unum

"Darren is a master showman. His knowledge of the event industry and his team's ability to reinforce a client's true program objectives has been demonstrated many times over. In his book, he has laid out a thoroughly comprehensive guide to achieve targeted success through event planning. I personally have been witness to his magic and the positive effects of his creative work. He has always been a big picture guy with great ideas. However, mastering the details outlined here is why his ideas work so well in practice."

S. Drew Toth
30 year hospitality veteran for
leading hotels around the world

GOING LIVE:
INSIDER SECRETS
TO CORPORATE
EVENT
PRODUCTION

How to Minimize Risks, Avoid Hidden Disasters, and Run a Smooth, Successful Event...Every Time!

Darren W. Johnson

Dudley Court Press, LLC
Sonoita, AZ

Copies of this book are available at special discounts for bulk purchases for educational, promotional or corporate use. Contact the publisher for more information.

Published in the United States of America by
Dudley Court Press, LLC
PO Box 102
Sonoita, AZ 85637
www.DudleyCourtPress.com
520-329-2729

Publisher's Cataloging-in-Publication Data
Johnson, Darren W.
Going live : insider secrets to corporate event
production / Darren W. Johnson. – Sonoita, AZ :
Dudley Court Press, c2013.

p. ; cm.
ISBN: 978-0-9831383-4-1 (hardback) ; 978-0-9831383-3-4 (pbk.)
"How to minimize risks, avoid hidden disasters, and run a smooth, successful
event ... every time!"
Summary: The key dos and don'ts for spectacular events. From planning to clean-up, the author covers all the critical information you need to succeed in the business, blending real life stories with insider tips and master strategies for anyone involved in the event planning and hospitality industries.–Publisher.

1. Business entertaining–Planning. 2. Business entertaining–Management. 3. Business entertaining–Production and direction. 4. Special events–Planning. 5. Special events–Management. 6. Special events–Production and direction. 7. Entertainment events–Planning. 8. Entertainment events–Management. 9. Entertainment events–Production and direction. 10. Special events industry-Handbooks, manuals, etc. 11. Hospitality industry–Handbooks, manuals, etc. 12. Public relations–Handbooks, manuals, etc. I. Title.

GT3405 .J65 2013
394.2/068–dc23   1304

ISBN 978-0-9831383-3-4 (paperback)
ISBN 978-0-9831383-4-1 (hardcover)

Printed in the United States of America

Book design by Gibson Creative Services

Darren & Karen

For my wife, Karen, my best
friend, soul mate, and the calm
in my never-ending storm. You
are my favorite thing in life.

ACKNOWLEDGMENTS

This book is a true testament to the fact that if I can write a book, anyone can. For all those people out there who think they may have a story to tell, just do it. It's not as hard as you think.

Karen, you are always there for me and have endured more than any one person should ever have to. There has been smooth sailing, not-so-smooth sailing, and even hurricanes (literally), but you have always kept me and our family together like no other woman could. Thank you for your continued support in my serial entrepreneurism and for the steady push to get this book done. This would have never happened and I could not have done it without you.

Daughters—a dad is said to be truly blessed when God gives him a daughter. I must be really blessed because he gave me four of the most fun-loving, beautiful girls who have turned into awesome young women–Ashley, Lindsay, Olivia, and Bayley, thank you for dealing with all my crazy life, travel, and absenteeism over the years and always providing me with so much unconditional love.

A thirty-year career is a long journey by any standard, and I cannot think of a better career industry so well-suited for me. I'm profoundly grateful to have come across it all those years ago. I never would have discovered it had it not been for a few important people.

My early and first debt of gratitude goes to Ed Thal, who saw some glimmer of hope in a twenty-one-year-old, fresh out of the US Marine Corps. He decided that I might fit into a hole with no shape, so he hired me for my first job in this business. Ed not only taught me how to read a P&L statement, but also the difference between a rose and an anthurium.

In most people's career journeys, they are lucky to happen upon just one mentor. But along my particular trail, I was fortunate enough to blindly stumble upon two. The second was Fritz Lehman, who was a great business partner for many years, and who also taught me the skills it takes to manage people—both clients and employees.

A major shout-out goes to all the awesome vendors, hoteliers, travel, and incentive companies and clients I've worked with over the years—some of which I've been associated with for more than two decades. They have been with me through thick and thin, and still remain good friends today. To name a few would be an injustice to hundreds, but I do want to give special thanks to Paul Weidner and The Kirby Team; Tom, Mike, and The Party Guys; Lee Peyton; Dave Ball; Michael Gozik; John Ekin; Susan Leszcynski; and many, many others.

One of the many rewarding benefits of this job is that there is little distinction between work and play. Those of us in this business have a truly unique profession, in which we get to enjoy the journey as much as the destination. Two special ladies who have taught me more than I thought I was capable of learning and who have made it possible for me to enjoy the ride along the way are Jenny and Judy. The miles, the laughs, the events, and the learning have made the last twelve years absolutely the best.

My final thank-you is to the United States Marine Corps, for instilling in me a never-say-die mentality and teaching me that failure is not an option. Those four years did more to shape the person I am today than I ever thought was possible when I first signed on. It was one of the best decisions I ever made. Semper Fi!

To hire Darren for speaking engagements or workshops,
email karen@dwj-p.com.

www.darrenwjohnson.com

"If there is a 50/50 chance that something could go wrong, then nine times out of ten it will."
- Paul Harvey

TABLE OF CONTENTS

ABOUT THE AUTHOR

Darren W. Johnson, CSEP, is a former United States Marine and a seasoned veteran in the special event industry. Having more than three decades of experience, he has produced live events throughout North America and the Caribbean. He has worked with hundreds of industry giants, including Disney, Shell Oil, Universal Studios, Coca-Cola, and Microsoft. With more than four thousand events produced in practically every imaginable location—deserts to tropical islands and ballrooms to airplane hangars—he is an experienced industry expert. Darren's work at major sporting events includes the Daytona 500, the Super Bowl, and PGA golf tournaments.

He has appeared on FOX, ABC, CBS, and NBC affiliates nationwide and been featured in Yahoo! Finance, the *Miami Herald*, and CBS MoneyWatch. Darren also speaks on event management at the University of Central Florida's Rosen College of Hospitality Management.

As the founder and executive producer of Darren W. Johnson Productions Inc., he created a number of companies under his brand, including Creative Services Event Company (CSEC), Tailgateville, and the Extreme Party Truck (XPT). As a full-service event management and production company, CSEC specializes in strategic planning, design, and execution of corporate events, sporting event hospitalities, and public event production. Tailgateville provides professional tailgating services at major sporting events and concerts. The Extreme Party Truck is the world's first complete mobile entertainment complex.

Darren coauthored a recently released book titled *The Success Secret* with *New York Times* bestselling author Jack Canfield, cocreator of *Chicken Soup for the Soul*.

To learn more about Darren W. Johnson visit www.DarrenWJohnson.com or e-mail info@dwj-p.com.

INTRODUCTION

"It's kind of fun to do the impossible"

– Walt Disney

Dinner was over; it was 8:45 p.m.—go time. The game show set rocked, complete with multitiered platforms, illuminated point counters, and a large digital scoreboard in the ballroom of the Atlantis Hotel on Paradise Island, in the Bahamas. All the lights, bells, and whistles were set, and the contestants—approximately 175 of my client's top producers—waited with excitement. These highly paid, commissioned salespeople, all extremely competitive alpha personalities, couldn't wait to battle for a shot at the big prize money.

The CEO introduced our show's host for the night, Bob Guiney (Bachelor Bob from ABC's *The Bachelor* TV show), and we called up the first batch of contestants. Bob was awesome, the rounds went off without a hitch, and we gave away a good chunk of cash. We also set up a lounge area for anyone who wanted to hang out and take photos with or talk to Bob after the show. He was a true professional and really went the extra mile to make the client happy. The entire crowd stayed through the whole event, and my client was thrilled. All in all, it was a smashing success.

The logistics involved in planning this event for my client, a nationally known insurance company, were extensive. Coming up with an event that would appeal to the twenty-five to thirty-five-year-olds who had won this incentive trip was the first step. Events in previous years had fallen flat; the client wanted to change things up and do something different on the final night of the trip. At our first brainstorming session, the management team expressed their frustration about not getting a good return on investment (ROI) in previous years. In other words, for what they spent on the event, the attendance had been disappointing. It was time for something new. Once we settled on the game show idea, my job was to make it happen.

Fast-forward six months. We had spent hours and hours building the set, incorporating the technology, creating and modifying the game rules, and finding a game host. We selected the right questions and answers and explored all the possible things that could go wrong when we operated the game. Now it was time to pack up all the equipment, technology, show set, and gear; load it into a container; put it on a boat; and send it to the Bahamas. I don't know if any of you have ever shipped things internationally, but it is always scary. Many things can happen along the way, like having your container fall off the ship into the ocean. That has happened!

Although everything arrived safe and sound, we still weren't out of the woods. On the evening of our game show, we had a very tight window for setup and rehearsal. The company held its daytime meeting in the same room as the dinner and game show. We were only allowed four hours to build the entire set and two hours to do the complete tech rehearsal. I'm talking about using this huge game show set, right off the ship, for the very first time, and hoping that all the electronics worked. Needless to say, I was a bit anxious.

The setup went painfully slow. We had to deal with one issue after another: screwed-up risers, power issues, and misbehaving electronics. Four hours to set up was extremely ambitious. We needed an entire day for setup and tech rehearsal, plus a couple of hours with Bob and our crew to go through the system and scoring. Although we completed the rehearsal with things still not functioning at 100 percent, we were able to fix the issues backstage during the dinner. As you already know, the event went off without a hitch. Such is show biz and the business of event production; you have to learn to make it work with what you have.

GAME SHOW (PHOTO BY DWJ)

So what, exactly, is event production? Today, the term "event production" is an extremely broad umbrella that encompasses everything from public events (fairs, festivals, concerts, sporting events, and races) to social events (weddings, birthdays, bar and bat mitzvahs, anniversaries, graduations, and fundraisers) to corporate events. We can further distill corporate events to trade shows, seminars, workshops, brand-to-consumer events, and more. Events can reward employees, thank customers, launch new products, build brand awareness, and connect with consumers. In fact, the last four decades have seen the event planning business explode. What used to be local mom-and-pop operations have become national and even multinational corporations, creating a multibillion-dollar industry. You will find a glossary in the back of the book to help define some of the terms and phrases used in this industry.

According to information provided by the Convention Industry Council (www.conventionindustry.org), approximately 1.7 million people work in the meetings and events industry in the United States alone. This does not include employees of the estimated three thousand recreational clubs (golf, yachting, athletic, town, and military) that regularly put on events. Nor does it include the many corporate employees pressed to produce some type of company function. Their numbers may never be tallied, but could easily reach the hundreds of thousands. Over 500 universities currently offer classes and degrees in hospitality management. College students involved in those programs add to the number of people entering the event industry. The social market could easily exceed several million event producers if we include all the individuals who plan weddings, birthdays, graduations, anniversaries, tailgate parties, and a multitude of special events.[1]

More and more companies are producing events, and that's a good thing. Local small and medium-size businesses conduct grand openings, customer appreciation events, employee recognitions, and big sales. However, a lot of people producing those events aren't qualified to do so. They're setting themselves and their organizations up for a potential disaster. They may know brand strategies or core values, but they lack knowledge in the world of event production. They may even be missing the event's goal, which leads to a waste of time and money, and potential embarrassment. A lot of folks out there can benefit from the expertise of a corporate event professional, and it's not only the big boys. Regional companies, local companies, and mom-and-pop businesses all put on events and may not have the expertise to do it successfully.

I can make two quick references to illustrate my point. First is a house painter. You can paint your house yourself, or you can hire a professional painter. Everyone knows when you painted it yourself. The corners, trim, and windows typically have smudged paint lines and crooked edges, versus a professional paint job that has perfect edges, trim, and windows. The same goes for photography; anyone can take pictures, but do they ever look as good as those by a professional photographer? Probably not. The same goes for putting on an event; anyone can do it, but will it be as good as one put on by a professional? Probably not.

If you have picked up this book, you probably have an appetite for event production or have executed some events already. Make no mistake; this may seem all wonderful and glorious when the event is a smashing success, but when it goes south, you'd better not be faint of heart. There will be storms, missed flights, power outages, equipment

1. Source: Convention Industry Council, www.conventionindustry.org (2011)

failures, and just plain ol' incompetent people that will try to trip you up.

This is where I come in. After more than thirty years of planning and executing thousands of complex events for Fortune 500 companies, I've learned what it takes to produce a great event that's memorable for all the right reasons. Whether you're planning a recognition dinner, corporate hospitality at a sporting event, new product launch, or any other intricate get-together, let my expertise be your guide. The helpful facts and insights on the pages that follow may prevent your event—and your hard-earned reputation—from becoming memorable for all the wrong reasons.

The purpose of this book is to help you navigate the minefield of potential disasters and unforeseen mishaps, enabling you to run a smooth, successful event every time. If you plan for every detail that could possibly derail your event, you will achieve success. If you prepare to the best of your ability, you will be ready when the unexpected happens. Time and experience are the best teachers, but hopefully I can spare you some of the experience by sharing my stories and suggestions.

You will hear the term "client" often as you read through this book. I use that term loosely; it does not refer only to someone who is paying you to produce an event. The reality is that whomever you are producing an event for is your client. It could be your own company, your dad, your town council, or an international charity. Paid or not, you should always think of the person or company desiring the event as a client. The only time you do not is when you are producing an event for yourself.

I've seen and learned a lot, including one indisputable, troublesome truth: Things do not always go as planned in the live event world. Millions of everyday people plan parties for birthdays, weddings, and anniversaries–professional producers work in the travel and event industries. They all will eventually be faced with the fact that things can, and often do, go wrong. It is a sure bet that at some point, your event will come face-to-face with a potential or actual disaster.

YOUR SUCCESS OR FAILURE WILL NOT BE MEASURED BY THE INCIDENT ITSELF, BUT BY HOW QUICKLY YOU RECOVER FROM IT.

There are three extremely important things to keep in mind as you read this book:

1. The devil is in the details. Plan, confirm, and reconfirm. The better the front-end planning, the easier the on-site execution. You will avoid a lot of drama when it counts.

2. Always have a back-up plan–more drama avoidance!

3. Loyalty is always your best resource. I mean that when the shit hits the fan, you may have to go to your vendors for instant help—a resolution or a fix. Those vendors you have treated loyally and fairly will be there to save your bacon. Don't be a "low bid always wins" producer. Nurture relationships. I have been using some of the same vendors for twenty years, through thick and thin. Together we've gone through big budgets, no budgets, and hurricanes—literally. When you need a favor (and believe me, you will), those are the people you can depend on.

If you take these three important points to heart, you will be on the road to successful event production. Although you may never have to face circumstances like the ones listed here, take a moment to consider what you would do in each of the following real-world situations.

Scenario 1: One hour before the opening welcome reception on the hotel's pool deck, big black clouds are building to the west. You know your client is emphatic about being outside, since this group from the Midwest has dug out of the snow to get to sunny Florida for their event. Do you chance it and hope the storm goes around you, or do you move the party inside and leave most of the beautiful décor and event elements outside—things that your client paid for?

Scenario 2: Forty-five minutes into your event, everything is going great. People are flowing in nicely, the vibe is good, the weather is perfect, and everybody's schmoozing and hitting the buffet lines hard. Then the caterer tells you he is almost out of food—and half the guests have not even arrived yet!

Scenario 3: You are running the most spectacular event of your life on Golden Beach. The client is elated because the ideal sunset has just happened right in front of her attendees' eyes. To make things even more perfect, the biggest full moon anyone has ever seen rises up over the horizon. But with it comes the highest of high tides. The extreme tide has snuck up on everyone, and now the rushing surf is washing up under the guest tables, buffets, and bars—which have no other place to go but out to sea.

Scenario 4: This is the final-night gala and awards ceremony. You have just pulled off three amazing events for an important, high-profile company. The food service was impeccable, the awards presentation went off without a hitch, and now all that's left is your closing entertainment—a popular comedian. As you stand in the back of the room with your client, who continues to receive compliments from her superiors for a job well done, the entertainer performs his routine. The performer seems to have really connected with the audience; everyone is laughing and having a ball. But as you and your client stand there basking in glory, you hear the beginning of a series of sexist jokes. Your client's satisfied expression changes to one of jaw-dropping anxiety. Suddenly, the taboo "F-bomb" lands with a resounding thud—and there is no place to hide!

Scenario 1: You double-check your weather radar for storm size and direction. Storm fronts are much easier to predict than pop-up thunderstorms. Remember that thunderstorms not only unleash buckets of rain, but the wind can also be disastrous and even deadly. Always try to err on the side of caution. Have an alternate location available in case the weather turns against you. I always remind the client, "I have never canceled a party that I moved inside." Remember that and use it!

Scenario 2: There are multiple issues about to unfold between you and the caterer. Don't debate or play the blame game. It has always been my position to implement the fix ASAP; deal with the cost and why it happened after the event. Nothing good will come from a twenty-minute confrontation over who is right or wrong. Tell that caterer to call in more food immediately, even if they have to get it from the grocery store.

Scenario 3: A bit of humor can go a long way. State the obvious— that Mother Nature has played a mean trick on you. She's given you a beautiful full moon coupled with a lovely onshore breeze, creating an abnormally super-high tide, as seen with Hurricane Sandy. Let the guests know that you are making a few slight modifications to the dinner plans. In all likelihood, the crowd will embrace this bit of excitement with open arms. The key here is to look at the situation head-on and quickly realize that there are no fixes to this problem. Be truthful with your client; try to make the situation as lighthearted and enjoyable as possible. If people see you freak out, then they will freak out. Don't ever freak out!

Scenario 4: When you are backstage, just before your entertainer goes on, you must always tell your act, "No profanity, racial, sexual, or political jokes, ever." You may have told them ten times prior to the gig, but always repeat it right before they go on. Another option is to hold the balance of the payment until the gig is over. Lastly, add a qualifier to the act's contract. If he or she uses any of the forbidden topics in their performance, 100 percent of the payment will be forfeited. Today, with social media and the Internet, you can find multiple reviews to check this entertainer's performances. You can also post your own reviews after the event is over.

The preceding scenarios were drawn from my own experiences. They are party-and entertainment–related calamities because my forte is the fun side of meetings, incentives, and brand-to-consumer events. I produce the party, the recognition, and the thank-you portion of these events. This is typically the "nighttime, have a big time" part that follows the meeting, general session, or educational component of a main event.

My role in that capacity is similar to that of a construction general contractor. The responsibilities include hiring and coordinating everything from venue selections to décor, entertainment to menu planning, production to security and cleaning. I hire the best vendors for each respective task—vendors that can meet the event's goal and budget.

It's all about the art of planning and coordination. In many instances, corporate event production mimics Homeland Security. The FBI, CIA, NSA, and TSA each do their own thing, but also coordinate with one another. If nobody shares information, the result can be bad. The same thing can happen when a brand or corporation divides up responsibility for an event among multiple people or entities. As more folks become involved in designing and executing an event, things can become compartmentalized.

For instance, a communications company produces the media and content, another company determines logistics, and an advertising agency puts together the promotional campaign—all without consulting one another. When you get on-site at the event, everything is disjointed because the left hand didn't know what the right hand was doing. Colors don't match. The entertainment may not be appropriate for the setting. Essential elements have fallen through the cracks. Overall, the event is not nearly as effective as it could have been. Instead, bring everyone together regularly to update each party's responsibilities. Identify any early components that may be disjointed or not ideally suited for the event goals. It's much easier to intervene at this point than on-site at "go" time.

The goal of this book is to teach you the essential elements. If everyone reads from the same sheet of music, your next event will flow like a perfectly conducted symphony—from start to finish. I've tried to include everything I know about the art (believe me, there is as much art as there is science) of corporate event production. This includes my time-tested tips, tricks, and advice, as well as lingo, forms, and other materials designed to make your work as an event producer easier. I'll even tell you a few war stories that I hope will entertain you and serve as reminders (and in some cases, warnings!) as you plan your next event.

Let's get this party started!

Chapter 1

What Makes a Successful Event Planner

Another day, another party…

Throughout my thirty-year career, people have asked me hundreds if not thousands of times, "How did you get into this business?" When I started in 1982, there were no degrees or schools in event management; it wasn't even an industry yet. I remember all the times I tried to explain to my grandparents what I did for a living. They would always tell their friends I was a caterer. After explaining it to them time and again, I simply let them believe I was a caterer. They and all their friends just couldn't understand what I would be doing if it wasn't the food and booze.

Funny, my job hasn't changed all that much in thirty years, although the name of my job has changed a lot. All the different titles people have for the term "event planner" truly amaze me. Personally, I like the term "event producer." It sounds more masculine.

Here are a few of the more common new terms:

- **Chief Creative Officer**
- **Chief Party Officer**
- **Event Architect**
- **Event Producer**
- **Event Planner**
- **Party Planner**

The event production business attracts certain kinds of people. I generally see three personality types in this industry: the creative type, the anal-retentive detail type, and the adrenaline junkie type. While all three are important in event production, some succeed more than others. This success is usually because they have surrounded themselves with the other two types, who can cover their shortcomings.

EVENT PRODUCER PERSONALITY TYPES

☐ 1. *Creative type.* Usually very out-of-the-box thinkers, they display a passion for floral design, creative design, interior design, or fashion. They are great visionaries and usually love getting their hands dirty with some or all of the execution. They can see things others cannot and are also capable of changing their minds many times in the creative process. They can be fairly unorganized, not great with details and budgets, and financial train wrecks. They do not like pressure, and struggle with punctuality, conflict, and mishaps. Often their focus on design will trump practicality or common sense.

☐ 2. *Anal-retentive detail type.* These people take great notes, have pronounced administrative and organizational skills, and are very punctual and budget-conscious. They typically possess little or no creativity, struggle with vision, and need to see everything in full color prior to making a decision. Common sense always triumphs over design for this personality types. Round pegs go into round holes, square pegs go into square holes, and logic must prevail. Often the need to micromanage and evidence of sleepless nights may be found in these individuals.

☐ 3. *Adrenaline junkies.* These individuals are typically unaffected by pressure or deadlines, sleep well at night, and show few signs of wear. They may overlook details, but they rarely lack ideas. Thankfully, their feelings do not get hurt easily. Creativity and enthusiasm are often hallmarks of this type, and they typically rise to all challenges—good and bad. These people will usually find a way to overcome all obstacles. Fiscal discipline will waver from time to time, as will common sense. However, decisions, opinions, and a "get-'re-done" mentality will prevail.

If you are one of these three personality types, then continue to read. Personal experience shows that all three types are needed to produce successful events. No matter which one you are, you will need the other two for success. Over time, you will learn and acquire the traits and skills of the other two. Until that happens, you need to find your other two mates. Sometimes you find a person that has more than one of these personality traits and skill sets, but they are pretty rare. I myself am definitely the number three. When I learned how important that special individual is, I hired the number ones and number twos. Over the years, I gradually improved my administrative and organizational aspects; through osmosis, I got better with the creative stuff.

All three personality types must also share another important characteristic. The one characteristic, whether learned or instinctual, is spontaneous decision making under pressure. It will be part of the job, whether you work in the office or out in the field. Initially the necessity will intimidate you, but it gets easier and less stressful the longer you do it. Approach your event with the intent of discovering what can go wrong before it happens. If you have all those bases covered, your rate of success will improve dramatically.

It's kind of masochistic, but I actually play out in my mind what I would do if X, Y, or Z were to happen. It has become a game for me. When I share these what-ifs with my wife, she looks at me like I'm crazy. And that's okay. I know that one of the reasons I've been so successful as an event producer is precisely because I think that way. I not only look for a potential problem, but also a viable solution to the problem. The solution to the problem is what I call the *art of recovery*.

THIS IS WHY YOU HIRE A PROFESSIONAL (PHOTO BY DWJ)

The Art of Recovery

Recovery is something that you definitely get better at with experience. I believe it is more art than science, and requires a different solution each time based on many changing variables. It requires thorough preproduction planning, fast thinking, and quick decision making when things go wrong. It also requires a bit of luck. When producing a live event, whether it's Junior's birthday party in the backyard or the President's Club gala dinner, there are numerous things that can go wrong. Many of these will be out of your control. Your ability to salvage the event when it goes sideways will determine not only the event's success, but also whether or not you keep your job.

For example, I once produced an event at a beach hotel for a major sponsor of the Daytona 500. It was scheduled to take place after a late-afternoon race, and traffic was in complete gridlock. One hour before the event, the band called and informed me that they had gone to the wrong hotel. They would not make it to my event because of the distance and traffic. There was no time to book another band, and having no entertainment at a party is hard to cover up. Fortunately, they were just going to be background entertainment.

Here is where the combination of quick thinking and luck came into play. I sent two of my staff down the beach, one in each direction, to look for a band playing in a hotel lobby or bar. We found one and offered them triple what they were making playing in the bar. Our crew moved all their gear and had them hooked up and in place when the doors opened for my client's event. Needless to say, the other hotel wasn't very happy with me, so I reimbursed them for the hijacked band. It ended up costing me four times what it should have, but my actions solved the problem. When those things happen, you have to put the financial aspects of the rescue out of your mind; you do whatever it takes to fix it. You can make the money back another day, and at least you will still have a satisfied client.

Recovery isn't always perfect, but when disaster strikes, stay calm and focus. I live by the old Barnum & Bailey Circus mantra: "the show must go on." It has sustained me for three decades in this business. So develop the mindset that you will make things work no matter what, come hell or high water, and pass that philosophy on to everyone on your team. Failure is not an option in this business because, like I said, there are no do-overs.

When a problem arises or a miscommunication with a vendor happens, do not waste your time and energy in the blame game. Instead, focus on the fix; you can unravel where the breakdown happened after you get the problem resolved. Every second counts when disaster strikes.

Remember...
- When an unexpected situation presents itself, embrace the opportunity to rescue the circumstance versus become part of the problem.
- You will have a much softer landing from an unforeseen incident if you have spent the proper time in the planning process. You cannot overestimate the value of pre-event planning.
- Always stay calm and focus. Sometimes solutions are very obvious.

Chapter 2

What Makes a Successful Event

"The noblest art is that of making others happy."

— *P. T. Barnum*

Most television shows are taped and then shown later. That way, producers can bleep or edit out any type of mishap, profanity, or incident. Even shows that are billed as "live" usually have a tape delay to bleep out profanity or cut the unforeseen wardrobe malfunction.

Unfortunately, with live events, you cannot edit, bleep out, or do-over. When the shit hits the fan, the lights go out, the skies open up, or the entertainer goes haywire, you'd better have a contingency plan. If not, the whole event could go up in smoke— and you with it. Therefore, you must plan, organize, and implement.

The first and most important task when producing an event is to determine the goal of the gathering. Why does the client want to have this event? What is the mission? Is it to entertain? To inform? To reward? To motivate? Likely it will be a combination of at least two of these, but there must be one overarching reason for it. You must keep that main reason or goal in mind as you progress through the planning stages.

Let's talk about the most common types of corporate events, with some explanation.

Appreciation Event – A company hosts or creates an event that thanks customers, employees, or volunteers for their patronage, support, and loyalty. These programs allow an event host to spend informal time with the guests in a non-traditional environment. Both parties have an opportunity to build a rapport and learn more about mutual business priorities. There are limitless possibilities and types of appreciation events that organizations hold throughout the year. Common programs include a large party with entertainment, dinner and theater, or suites at sporting events.

A plain, simple "thank you" has a truly amazing impact. You know exactly what I am talking about. When you purchase a product or service and the salesperson tells you, "Thank you for your business; we really appreciate it," you feel good. All too often, businesses forget this simple but powerful act. Appreciation events provide an environment for ownership or management to thank their customers or employees in a casual, disarming atmosphere. It is extremely important that the vibe and the venue are conducive to mixing and mingling. Usually this would be a stand-up event that allows people to move about easily and have multiple interactions throughout the course of the night. The last thing you want is a lot of seating, where everyone plops down and doesn't interact. Keep the volume down, too, if any entertainment is present. Follow up with a handwritten thank-you card after the event and say it one more time.

Employee Recognition Event – A company recognizes employees or rewards them for outstanding accomplishments. Coworkers, spouses, and guests typically attend these events. Company executives present the awards and speak about each employee's achievements. Recognition events are hosted at either a

EMPLOYEE RECOGNITION EVENT (PHOTO BY DV PIX)

EMPLOYEE RECOGNITION EVENT (PHOTO BY DARREN W. JOHNSON)

company's facility or off-property at a location with an upscale setting. This type of event usually includes dinner, beverages, and entertainment.

Let's ask ourselves, what would make this a successful event? When hosting this type of event, you want the people being recognized to feel appreciated. You want them to feel the love. It is very easy to put on an event like this and completely miss the target. It is extremely important that you make the recognition feel genuine and thoughtful, not factory-like and impersonal. Having the ownership or management present the award with a handshake and congratulations goes a long way. Reinforce the appreciation to the employees with management face time before or after the ceremony. They can have simple conversations about their families, hobbies, pets, or any number of other topics. These things cost absolutely nothing besides time, and create more goodwill than you can imagine.

Executive Retreats and Incentive Programs – Corporations spend big bucks at these events on a per-person basis. Often held at luxury resorts in exclusive destinations, they receive the most visibility in an organization. Topics on the agenda usually include business development and organizational planning. Executive retreats and incentive trips typically last between three and five days, and require attention to site selection, lodging, transportation, catering, business meetings, golf, and other activities. Negotiation skills must be sharp, because these programs involve all aspects of event planning. Employee recognition and customer appreciation events are commonly held during these incentive programs.

Executive retreats are generally created for corporate leadership teams. They are held in locations that eliminate potential interruptions of the leadership's daily job responsibilities. These locations need to be conducive to meetings that are free of distractions and inspire free thinking. In this way, their agendas of business development and organizational planning can be put into discussion.

What does it take to create a successful incentive program? First, you need a healthy budget. Before the concept of an incentive program is ever announced, planners must research the costs associated with implementing these programs. Hundreds of companies specialize in incentive programs, using both merchandise and travel as incentives. Due to the complexity of implementing these programs, corporations should engage the services of a specialist. In my experience, these programs are hugely successful and can provide tremendous ROIs. One word of advice: It is always better to provide a nicer shorter trip than a longer second-rate trip. People remember quality—good or bad.

Brand-to-Consumer Event – This is often referred to as a type of experiential marketing event. The term "experiential marketing" refers to actual customer experiences with the brand, product, or service that drive sales and increase brand image and awareness. It's the difference between telling people about features of a product or service, and letting them experience the benefits for themselves. Experiential marketing allows consumers to personally engage and interact with products, brands, and services. This sensory interaction allows them to have a personal experience with the product being presented. Personal experiences help people connect to a brand and make intelligent, informed purchasing decisions. When done right, it's the most powerful tool out there to win brand loyalty.

MORTGAGE COMPANY ENGAGING POTENTIAL HOME BUYERS (PHOTO BY DWJ)

JOHNSONVILLE BRATS SET-UP FOR CONSUMERS SAMPLING (PHOTO BY DWJ)

CONSUMERS SAMPLING JOHNSONVILLE BRATS (PHOTO BY DWJ)

Brand-to-consumer events can be as simple as cooking sausage on a grill and handing out samples. They can also be as complicated as a multicity tour touching thousands of people at each event. I have done both, and both are extremely effective. The biggest challenge when creating these events is that different markets can have completely different results. Therefore, when implementing this type of event, start with a pilot program. Choose at least two different cities or markets, and then determine your ROI from these events. This type of event is different from the others mentioned previously in one main respect: It is open to the public. As a result, determining the attendance or "flow-through" is difficult. A solid pre-event marketing budget is needed to ensure a respectable turnout. Without good attendance, it's difficult to make a knowledgeable determination regarding the event's effectiveness.

Seminars and Conferences – Organizations plan and hold these meetings with targeted audiences, and provide attendees with relevant information. Seminars are usually shorter events; they can last a couple of hours, half a day, or a whole day. They have single or multiple speakers, and they keep all of the attendees together in the same space. Conferences, on the other hand, typically have multiple, concurrent sessions. They are usually held at hotels, begin with a keynote session, and then hold breakout sessions by topic. A conference is generally planned for one day, two days, or sometimes longer.

The key to a successful seminar or conference is venue selection. Ensure that you select a venue conducive to learning; education is the reason people attend seminars and conferences. If you select a venue that is full of distractions—be it noise, gambling, construction, or geographic challenges—you are setting yourself up for failure. Always try to select a venue that will inspire thinking and learning. Provide quality audio-visual (AV) equipment for all presenters and marketers. It is extremely embarrassing to have the presenter's microphone cracking or popping, feedback screeching, or lighting malfunctioning. Have you ever been in a situation when the PowerPoint presentation was not available due to a burned-out bulb in the projector? There are numerous ways to encounter unwanted A/V mishaps, so try to get a good-quality vendor. Always get bids from companies other than the in-house provider, too. In-house A/V vendors typically pay an exorbitant fee back to the hotel for the privilege of being the "in-house" provider, and that fee is passed on to the customer.

Trade Shows – Organizations attend trade shows to generate leads. They can host them to reinforce their image or brand as an industry leader among those who attend. Attendees usually include organization members, customers, prospects, and suppliers. Event planning for trade shows involves negotiating trade-show booth rates, advertising and promotion at the event, and sometimes speaking opportunities. Many logistical details exist to assure that the trade-show booth, promotional materials, giveaways, and staff arrive on time for your company.

First and foremost, successful trade shows require highly motivated people who can interact with strangers at a moment's notice, over and over again. It takes very deliberate action to generate as many leads as possible. This lead generation is necessary to ensure that your ROI is achieved. Pre-event marketing is a great way to help ensure success. It lets many of your prospects know that you will be present at the show. You can also take that opportunity to give them your specific booth number. Your booth aesthetics—soft, cushioned carpet and a warm, inviting space—help to create a successful event. Think about it. You have just a few minutes to try to establish rapport with a prospect as he or she walks down the aisle, looking at booth after booth. Set yourself apart with a great attention-getter and clever giveaway. Very often companies will host events at night, after the show floor closes. They will invite people that they spoke to during the day. This provides for additional relationship building in hopes of turning a prospect into a new customer. I have seen a great many relationships developed after the show floor closes.

PHOTO BY GIE

PHOTO BY GIE

PHOTO BY GIE

No matter what specific type of event you will be producing, they all require certain steps, taken in a certain order. If you plan to produce a successful event, then you must follow these seven steps each and every time.

SEVEN STEPS TO A SUCCESSFUL EVENT

The seven fundamental steps in producing a successful event are the same whether you are in a backyard or a grand ballroom. These items may seem very basic and elementary, but they hold true for producing both social events and corporate events. Overlooking any one of these essentials could possibly undermine your entire event, so I recommend that you follow them closely every time. As you read through these steps, you will see how they are all interconnected. It is no different than a recipe for a cake—if you leave out one ingredient, the cake may still be good, but it won't be a killer. Here's to your next *killer* event!

▶ Step 1 – The Goal

Why are you having this event? This may seem obvious, but if you don't know *why* or if you don't have an end result in mind, you'll waste precious time and money. Without a clear understanding of what you or the client is trying to achieve, you also risk possible embarrassment. Don't get me wrong; it is perfectly fine to have a party with no purpose, as long as you know that going in. Events have a lot more continuity and impact when the purpose and the goal are clearly visible from beginning to end. The goal is the driver of all things; it will—or should—determine the following six items. The goal is the compass that will provide us with our direction.

▶ Step 2 – The Budget

Determine *exactly* how much money is allocated for this event. Sometimes this can be a difficult thing to determine. Often you don't have a budget laid out, so you try to skimp along during the planning process. Then the day before (or day of) the event, you realize all of the things that you don't have because you didn't want to spend the money. Instead of being embarrassed or looking like a cheapskate, you rush out and buy all of those things anyway. At that point, you usually end up with inferior products because you are shopping at the last minute. You have also spent a lot more money than necessary, because you couldn't comparison shop. Larger companies budget their events more effectively. They usually get their budgets from previous events or will allocate a specific budget to produce the event.

Sometimes you may not know how much to budget for your event. I suggest you create a detailed list of all the items (food, beverage, entertainment, rentals, etc.) that you would like to have, and collect those costs. Add all of those items up, and determine if you or your client can live with that number. If they can't live with that amount, separate the need-to-have items from the nice-to-have items, and work it from there. You are better off having fewer nice things than many cheap things.

Step 3 – The Location

Where are you going to host the event? This can and surely will impact the budget. You can usually narrow down your location options after you have determined your goal and budget for the event. It is rather difficult to host an event at Donald Trump's place if your budget is twenty dollars per person. You don't want to have an event at a location that is not conducive to your goal. If the goal is for your client's salespeople to interact with customers, then you don't want to be in a loud or noisy place. Or if you are having an employee recognition event, then you don't want to be in a venue that is chopped up. Lots of small rooms prevent everyone from sitting together and seeing the whole group.

Clients battle this the most when it comes to office parties. They may want to show off their fifth-floor office space, but it typically has no open areas for people to mingle. It's usually chopped up into a dozen smaller offices and conference rooms, making it impossible to create the right vibe with good interaction. Therefore, give a lot of consideration to your location after you have determined your client's goal. The fastest way to undermine the goal is to choose a location that does not fit the purpose.

Step 4 – The Vibe

The *vibe* is the mood or feel of the event. It is the intangible outcome of the combination of all your event's components: décor, seating, entertainment, location, and so on. The vibe has its own personality. Ask yourself, "Is this event going to be fun, themed, audience participatory, casual, or formal?" The answer to that question usually comes when you are addressing the event's goal. You must make sure that the goal and the vibe are compatible. For example, outdoor venues are not typically conducive to formal events. Think about it: Women hate sweating, having their hair messed up, and wearing high heels in grass. Fun events that include audience participation aren't usually held in places like offices, museums, or historical venues. Barns or airplane hangars are not common locations for an awards dinner. There is a reason for this. Professionally speaking, you can pull off any type of event in any venue once you gain experience, but for now, just work on matching the vibe with the goal.

Step 5 – The Food

How will you deal with food? Will it be catered? Is it sit-down, stand-up, or a plated (served) dinner? All of these things are tied together, and every one of them is determined by your goal. The first item to decide is the time of the event. This determines how heavy your food service will be. If you put on an event from 11:00 a.m. to 1:00 p.m., then you'd better have a real lunch, not just crudité, cheese, and crackers. If your event is from 6:00 p.m. to 8:00 p.m., then plan on having enough food for dinner. I see this mistake made all the time; people have an event during a mealtime and only serve light snacks or horsd'oeuvres. Two things happen: 1) everyone gets drunk because they didn't eat enough, and 2) they leave in the middle of the event to get something to eat.

It is also important to serve the right type of food with the right event. If you are having a mixer where people are standing and mingling, don't serve food that requires cutting with a knife. Have you ever tried cutting into a piece of steak while holding your plate, drink, and fork? Of course you have, and you didn't like it, did you? Don't serve barbecue (aka.messy food) at formal events. And last, make sure that you provide nonmeat or nonseafood options. After all, many people have special dietary needs, limitations, and preferences.

Step 6 – The Beverages

Is there going to be alcohol served? Does it fit with your goal? Are you hosting the bar (paying for it), and if so, is it beer and wine or a full open bar? Are you using well brands, call brands, or premiums? Are you willing to take responsibility for the consequences if someone is overserved? Pay attention to how much your guests are drinking. It is always my recommendation to have someone (a professional) serving the drinks, versus allowing your guests to self-serve. Why? If you are hosting an event serving alcohol and someone overindulges, gets ill, causes some type of property damage, gets hurt, or worse, you could be liable. There are many issues to be aware of when it comes to serving alcohol. Always err on the side of caution and hire a professional.

Step 7 – The Entertainment

What entertainment options best fit the goal? If you are having a bunch of guys at an event, then a dance band probably isn't the right choice. Entertainment is not only driven by the goal, but also by your audience. Whether the audience is gender specific, young, not young, sales, operations people, and so forth, you need to know their likes and dislikes. Some groups want to sit and be entertained; some groups want to blow the roof off. Know your audience. It is extremely uncomfortable to see your entertainment completely flop.

Needless to say, entertainment is the one item that can severely impact your budget. If you can't afford live entertainment or a DJ, then at least get your iPod and a small sound system to have some background music. The single biggest mistake people make is not having some type of music at their event. It is difficult to get a good vibe going without it. It can be done for free and still have the same effect. Even the radio is better than silence.

By addressing these seven fundamental items, you can ensure a smooth, successful event, whether you're on the beach for a family reunion or at the Ritz for an awards ceremony.

Remember...

- Goal – Determine why you are having the event and what you want to achieve.

- Budget – Decide how much you are willing to spend on your event. Make a list of need-to-have items and nice-to-have items.

- Location – Pick a venue that fits the goal.

- Vibe – Make sure your vibe fits the goal and the venue.

- Food – Select a menu appropriate for the time of day and also the vibe of the event.

- Beverage – Determine if alcohol fits with the goal. If so, is it beer and wine or a full bar? Is it a cash bar or a hosted bar?

- Entertainment – Make sure the entertainment is appropriate to the goal, and that you match the right entertainment with the right audience.

Chapter 3

Selecting and Inspecting Your Venue

"It's not the will to win that matters—everyone has that.
*It's the will **to prepare to win** that matters."*

— *Paul "Bear" Bryant*

When you're considering venues, not only do you have to think about the client's goal but also the size of your budget. Would an indoor or outdoor event be better for this particular mission? You must consider the type, size, and configuration of each space you encounter in your search for the perfect venue. Let's say you decide an indoor location is best this time. Is the site chopped up into small rooms, or is there a large open space? Does it have an outside area? Is it suitable for a cocktail reception and a dinner? Is there an area that can be used as a central focal point for an awards presentation or a keynote address?

Maybe you decide to go with an outdoor location instead. If you select a location because it has a beautiful outdoor space, make sure there is also sufficient interior space nearby. You'll need it to hold the gathering if the weather doesn't cooperate. I've seen it happen many times before; people hold an event outdoors, and then they don't have anywhere to go when it rains. That consideration is as important as any other part of the selection process when considering outdoor spaces. So you actually have to plan for two events—the original one outdoors, and the Plan B one inside. Also think about the ground surface. Is it suitable for the way your guests will be dressed? For example, if your event is the least bit formal, can women in high heels walk on that surface with no problems?

DARREN'S TIP Even if you fall in love with a space, it might not have the functional working elements necessary to achieve your goal. You may need to consider a less appealing option that does achieve your goal.

Site Inspection

Once you know why you're having the event and have found a space that you think meets your needs, it's time to visit the site in person. An advance visit will not always be possible—sometimes the client will secure the space first, and you'll be forced to work with what you've got. But let's assume that you're going to have the luxury of choosing the space yourself, and you are able to do an advance site visit.

Here is a nutshell description of what you need to do:

- Take pictures of every part of that venue. They don't have to be professional quality photos; just whip out a digital camera or your phone and start shooting everything—even the bathrooms. These photos will help down the road when you're doing the actual planning, but they're also important to show to the person who is paying you to produce the event.

- You must also have accurate measurements of the doors. It's absolutely amazing how often event planners overlook the issue of how they will get all of their décor, equipment, and people, as well as any oversized items, inside a building. An oversized item is typically an object your client rented or had custom created. It could be a giant eight-foot tall welded sculpture of the world that rotates and shows where all the corporate offices are located, which has been fabricated in one piece. Your event is in a 10,000 square-foot room, and it never dawns on you to measure the doors. Don't become a statistic; measure the height and width of all doorways.

- Measure the room's dimensions so you can make sure all of the elements needed to produce your event are going to fit. The stage, the dance floor, all the tables, the bar, the buffet line, production control—all these things require space. Eyeballing it is a terrible idea. Don't ask me how I know this.

- It's equally important to measure ceiling heights. Let's say that instead of measuring, you take the venue's word for it when they tell you the ceiling is twenty feet high. Based on that information, you have an eighteen-foot-tall stage set custom built for the event. Big bucks. You get the set inside the building on *game day* with no problem (you *did* measure the doors!), only to find that the part of the room where the stage is supposed to go has a soffit that drops down four feet. And *voila!* Your twenty-foot ceiling is suddenly a sixteen-foot ceiling –and your stage set is too tall. Chainsaw, anyone?

 Always measure the entire ceiling, paying special attention to soffits, hanging light fixtures, and air-conditioning ductwork throughout the space.

- Next is the acoustics. While you're in there measuring, make note of the ceiling, wall, and floor surfaces, because they'll determine what kind of acoustics you're going to be dealing with. Carpeted floors, carpeted walls, and insulated ceilings make for good acoustics. Large spaces like airplane hangars or museums, and rooms with hard floors, hard walls, and tall ceilings, make for less-than-ideal acoustics.

- How about the electrical power–is it safe and sufficient for your needs? Electrical is one of the most overlooked issues in event production, especially at older venues. And it's not a problem until you are out of it! Then suddenly the circuit breakers pop, the place goes dark, the band goes dead, and "Houston, we have a problem."

- Is there enough parking, or will you have to shuttle people down the road to and from a parking lot?

- Is there a kitchen on the premises, or will the caterers have to bring their own kitchen? Is there refrigeration? Is there potable water?

- Will you have to use elevators to get supplies and equipment to the upper floors? Elevators can be a nightmare if you have to use them to take supplies and décor to the top floor and the stuff you're taking doesn't fit in the elevator. When dealing with elevators, always measure twice.

- Finally, when doing your venue inspection, don't forget to ask all the seemingly silly questions that you can think of. Find out: Are there lots of bugs at night? Are there any issues with the plumbing? Is the surrounding area safe at night? Any other special events or construction close by that might impact the event? Are there any unusual, less obvious rules or circumstances that we need to know about?

"Well, yeah, you have to turn the band off at nine because the city has a moratorium on noise after nine." Wow, good to know! And you might never have uncovered that little tidbit had you not asked about a noise curfew. You'll be surprised at all of the hidden gems venue manager will tell you about, if you only ask.

After you have chosen a specific venue, there is one more step you can take to boost the odds that your event will be successful: a CAD.

The Importance of Drawing Your Space

Today, almost every event I produce requires a computer-aided design (CAD), showing the location of every item that is going into the event space. In today's world, special events have become much more of a common occurrence. Every municipality's fire department has various codes relating to what is acceptable from a layout in a specific venue. In most cases, with larger events, a CAD is required by the local fire marshal to ensure proper egress (emergency evacuation), resolve fire-safety issues, and ensure that no fire sprinklers are blocked or interfered with. CADs are not only required by local fire departments but are also an essential tool for all vendors, suppliers, and staff working on an event because they show exactly where every item should go. It is the sheet music that all should be singing from. CAD software packages are readily available today and are easier to use than ever before. The most commonly used, for the greatest detail, is VectorWorks. It's update regularly with new icons, symbols, and event equipment drawn to scale.

In fact, I now draw a CAD whenever I consider a space for an event, just to ensure everything will fit and that I can accomplish the event's goal there. This practice has paid off more than once. On many occasions, even though we fell in love with particular spaces, the preliminary CADs proved that the event components would not fit. Before we had CADs, we discovered that sad truth the hard way.

If you were wondering whether or not I actually generate the CADs myself, the answer is no. I have neither the patience nor the desire to learn the program. Instead, I print out a diagram of the event space, hand-draw the stuff on it, scan it, and send it to my CAD guy. Once we get the basics in, we make adjustments either over the phone or via e-mail. Pretty simple.

DARREN'S TIP Get yourself a good CAD guy. Their fees are very reasonable, and you will look like a pro.

Once you have laid out the event in a way that provides for smooth guest flow and the achievement of your event's goal, you'll send the layout to the venue. They will make the comments, changes, or additions.

After all the involved parties have made their changes to the CAD, you will most likely have to submit the drawing to the fire marshal for final approval. Sometimes the venue has to send the final drawing, and sometimes you, as the producer, are responsible for sending it. Fire codes vary from city to city, and the fire marshal's word is the gospel. Service doors, corridors, emergency exits, and such are commonly noted on the CAD. Fire marshals are most concerned with egress and any potential fire hazards from electrical services, open flames, fire-retardant fabric, and items or hazardous materials stored on-site. Accommodating the fire marshal's needs may require that some items be moved.

Here are a two examples of CAD drawings.

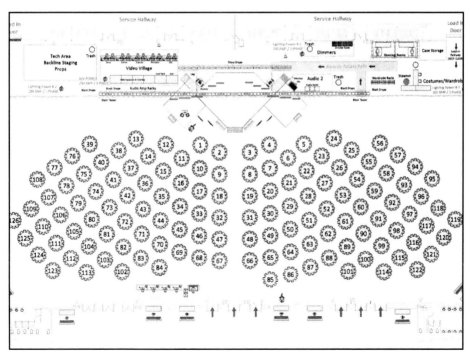

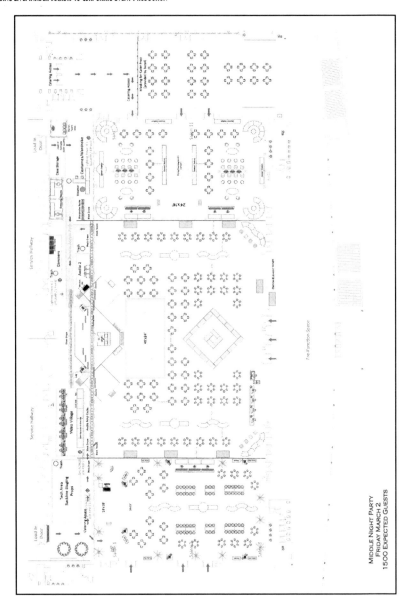

MIDDLE NIGHT PARTY
FRIDAY MARCH 2
1500 EXPECTED GUESTS

CADs have been a great addition to the event industry. They're a terrific way to get everyone—the client, the venue, the production, the fire marshal, and so on—on the same page. Don't fight them; embrace them. They are a valuable tool that can help you do your job more effectively.

Another way that CADs make you effective is by helping you to examine the chosen venue's electrical power. As we mentioned earlier, sufficient power is vital to your event's success.

Scotty, Give Me More Power

You may have heard the phrase above coming from Captain James T. Kirk on the starship *Enterprise* whenever he needed more power to push the spaceship past warp speed. Power is one of the most critical elements of any event, but it's only critical when you don't have enough of it. Lessons about power are usually learned the hard way. I want to try to help you avoid some of *that* potential pain and suffering.

When doing events in hotels, power is usually readily available—expensive, but available. At other venues, one of the first questions I always ask is, "How much power do you have?" The good news with power is that if you don't have much of it at your site, it's easy to bring in more. You will spend additional money when bringing in power, but bringing in any element costs money, whether it's restrooms, catering facilities, or whatever. The trick is understanding your power requirement from the beginning, so you can budget for it and bring in enough to get the job done.

The biggest mistake people make when it comes to power is trying to utilize only what's already in the venue. But once the event begins, guess what? It turns out that there wasn't enough to go around after all. Older locations are notorious for not having enough power. You may see plenty of wall outlets and think that you're good to go. You plug in and everything's fine for a while. Then the caterers arrives (they're usually the last ones in) and they start plugging in the heat lamps they use to keep the food warm, the waffle makers, the panini makers…and all of a sudden, *bang!* You're in the dark.

Yes, you had a bunch of outlets, but they were probably all tied to the same circuit. If you plug items into each of those outlets, I guarantee that something is going to give. Circuits are going to blow, and then you will have a much bigger issue on your hands. The lights go off, the band gets shut down, and everything else that was running on power goes offline, too. It is not only embarrassing when that happens, but also a major headache. Often you have to call in the venue's engineering staff or someone else to turn the breakers back on—or to even locate the breaker panels to begin with.

DARREN'S TIP   Never skimp on power. It's one of those things that will bite you every time. If budget constraints are forcing you to compromise on certain elements of your event, compromise on something other than power.

Diesel generators are quiet now compared to the old, noisy, gas-powered ones that tainted so many events in the past. Just make sure that your generator has enough fuel to last for the duration of the event. And remember, you're not only contracting for the power itself (the generator), but you also have to order the distribution. That includes all the cabling and boxes it takes to run the power from wherever the generator is sitting to the precise location(s) in the venue. I'm not talking about dollar-store extension cords here. I'm talking big, heavy cables with the distribution boxes for plugging in all of your elements. Hire a good, reliable generator company, and let that person make it all happen.

Here's a funny generator story:

Once I produced a multiday event at a hotel in Bermuda. One of the events was on the beach. There weren't a lot of generators available on the island of Bermuda, but I made sure I rented the biggest one I could find. I have the mindset that, when it comes to power, you can never have too much.

The day before our beach event was supposed to take place, a transformer or something major at the island's main power substation blew up. Suddenly, half of the island was without power. Now, there I was with 350 people on an incentive trip at a resort in Bermuda, and the hotel was totally powerless. That meant no air-conditioning, no running water, no flushing toilets, no lights in the hallway, no cooking, no nada. This went on for a day and a half. It was unbelievable. You would have thought that we were on Gilligan's Island or something. It was stifling hot, and everybody stayed in the swimming pool. And then there was me, with a huge generator chained up down at the beach for my event the next day.

BERMUDA BEACH PARTY
(PHOTO BY DWJ)

The generator people started calling; they needed me to return the generator. I told them there was no way I was giving my generator back. I had already paid for it and contractually owned the generator for the next three days. It got to the point where the government of Bermuda was even trying to get that generator. Imagine! You had grocery stores without power; everything in the freezers was melting and defrosting; everything under refrigeration was spoiling. You really have no idea how bad it is to lose power for that long, unless you've been through something like a hurricane.

Needless to say, I had a contract with my client to provide this beach event, regardless of whether or not the hotel or the country had power. Since I had the only generator that was going to make it work, I had to battle people for a day and a half to keep them from taking my generator away. It became a pretty big deal.

About two hours before our event was set to begin, the power came back on. We were able to do the big beach party with sufficient power for everything. It was a rather trying incident, but this is typical of the things that happen in the corporate event production world.

DARREN'S TIP As a corporate event producer, you have to learn to stand your ground and go with the flow at the same time. Easier said than done!

The next issue on power has to do with the planning phase of your event, when you're trying to calculate how much power you're going to need. Once you have identified all of the elements for the event—entertainment, decorations, lighting, bands, audio, video equipment, photo booths, catering, and so forth—have each supplier provide you with their power needs and calculate your total needs. You can then contact the venue and give them your power requirements. Request a quote in writing from their power provider or from the venue itself. This will give you a rough idea of what your potential power charges are going to be. Once you have completed your final CAD, be sure that you identify the location and quantity of each power drop that is required. You can then resubmit that drawing to the power provider, and who can give you a revised and exact quote for the power charges. If your event is going to be at a hotel, they'll have an in-house electrical contractor. His job is to take your power requirements and provide you with the power you need where you need it.

And now for the final word on power: cost. I recently completed a three-day event with a total electric bill of $17,000. Power is something that a venue can use as a profit generator. Always remember to ask for a power estimate prior to the event. Once the event has happened and you are gone, they can bill you for charges that you have no way of challenging if you didn't ask for an estimate. Never underestimate the cost, because it can be pretty substantial.

In addition to power, another issue that can sneak up on you, carrying potential for disaster and unforeseen costs, is the matter of restrooms.

The WC

WC is short for *water closet*, otherwise known as the restrooms. Although a lot of producers don't give them much consideration, quite a fiasco can result from insufficient quantities or malfunctions. I've produced numerous events at venues with restrooms that were less than adequate. Often, they were antiquated and ended up failing because of the heavy use that a private event puts on restroom facilities.

In many older venues, the bathrooms are simply insufficient. That's not a problem for the first two hours, but eventually you'll see a line of fifty women at the ladies room door; they're all going to be unhappy and let you know it. That's not good for the guests, for the event's goal, or for you as a producer. Don't let a lack of restrooms be your downfall.

For venues that are not typically used for corporate events (places such as warehouses, museums, or airplane hangars), always look at both the male and female restrooms. Are they upstairs or downstairs? Are they handicap accessible from the rooms in which your event is going to take place? Take pictures, count the stalls, and then do the math on how many bathrooms you think you'll need for that event.

DARREN'S TIP

It seems to me as if the WC need isn't quite as heavy for daytime events as it is for those held at night. If there is going to be a lot of drinking and dancing, restroom use will increases quite a bit, so keep that in mind.

If you find that there are just not enough stalls to accommodate your crowd, you'll have to bring in more. In that case, you have two choices: port-a-potties or restroom trailers. If it's an all-guy group, you may get away with the old standby port-a-potties, but women hate them. If your guest list includes females, consider the port-a-potties only as a last resort—and I mean a *very last* resort. I recommend bringing in restroom trailers instead. These can be anything from little two-stall men's and women's units that only cost a few hundred dollars to rent, to big, deluxe executive restroom trailers with air-conditioning, granite countertops, private stalls, running water (hot and cold), soap dispensers, towel dispensers, lighting, and mirrors. They are a terrific addition to an event with deficient facilities. It's very easy to bring them in, and it's worth the extra effort and expense. These units have self-contained holding tanks, but they do require water and electric to run, so you'll need power and a water source.

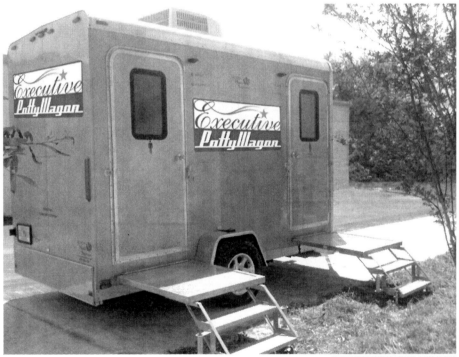

SMALL PORTABLE RESTROOM TRAILER (PHOTO BY DWJ)

Just make sure that no matter which kind of restrooms you're using, they are thoroughly cleaned prior to the event. Put some type of air fresheners in them, too. Anything you can do to enhance older, not-so-pretty bathrooms, do it. We typically add scented candles, florals, and nice hand towels to upgrade a restroom facility on the day of the event. You can even place potted flowers in the men's urinals if you have a women-only event and use both men's and women's restrooms.

Remember...

The benefit of the site inspection is to troubleshoot and avert potential disasters. You are doing this due diligence to make sure that the venue meets all of the requirements necessary to reach your client's goal. You simply cannot wing it. Take the time to connect the dots during your site inspection visit(s), and you'll be well on the road to a successful event. Remember the following points:

- Make sure the venue matches your event goal.

- If you select an outdoor venue, make sure you have an indoor or covered back-up space.

- Take lots of pictures during your site inspection.

- Measure the entire space, including ceiling height, doorways, and elevators.

- Create a CAD of your event in the venue prior to contracting.

- CADs can help you save time, money, and embarrassment by showing you in advance what will work inside a venue and what won't.

- Get a good CAD professional.

- Never cut corners when it comes to power. When in doubt, bring in generators.

- Be sure to rent the modern, quiet, diesel generators, not the older (loud!) gas types.

- Hire a reputable generator company to help you with both the power and the distribution.

- Don't underestimate a venue's power costs. They can blow your budget big-time.

- Always evaluate the restrooms for both genders during your site inspection.

- Evening events require more restrooms than daytime functions.

- Use port-a-potties only as a last resort when you are having female guests.

Chapter 4

Event Pre-planning Basics

"Never neglect details. When everyone's mind is dulled or distracted the leader must be doubly vigilant."

— Colin Powell

If you learn one thing from this book, it should be that your success as a producer or the success of an event is greatly increased if you spend a significant part of your time in the planning phase of the event. Don't just assume that your vendors are going to do it the proper way, that the weather is going to be perfect, and that the power is not going to fail. The devil is in the details, and you must think through as many contingency plans as you can in order to easily handle the inevitable mishap. In the pages that follow I have outlined the basics to the planning stage of producing an event. Everyone has his or her own style, format, or process; this is mine and has worked for the last thirty years.

The Proposal

The proposal is a sales document that you create for the client. It conveys the customer experience that your event is going to generate and how much it's going to cost. I have been creating proposals for thirty years, and I must admit that I am no creative writer when it comes to crafting these documents. When I first started out, I used to hand-write every proposal, have someone type it, and mail it to the client. Back then, a proposal was nothing more than a brief description of the items I would provide and a price. For large events, we might have included a rendering that showed our vision of what the event would look like.

Fast-forward thirty years, and *wow!* Proposal writing is now an art in itself. You can desktop publish a document that includes photos, video, and mp3 files for bands and entertainment. Creating a proposal for an event is similar to writing a book or magazine article—everyone has his or her own style. There is no longer a standard format. Everybody gets to choose for themselves how best to communicate the aesthetic components of the event. Producers also convey how the music will sound, how the food will be displayed, how the event will flow, and how the staging and production will look.

With that being said, the days of overly syrupy wordsmithing describing the "free-flowing, silk fabric swags gently fluttering in the breeze" are passé. People want to read about and understand the overall vibe of the event and items they are getting. All the excessive jargon used in past decades is obsolete and a waste of a producer or planner's time. No client wants to read all that mumbo-jumbo. A good, honest description followed by a photo and a price—that's what the best producers provide. Exactly how you present that is up to you and your style. But as a producer, I want the meat and not the sizzle.

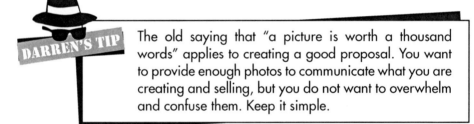

DARREN'S TIP   The old saying that "a picture is worth a thousand words" applies to creating a good proposal. You want to provide enough photos to communicate what you are creating and selling, but you do not want to overwhelm and confuse them. Keep it simple.

Every proposal should include the following components:

Event Title

If the event doesn't already have a name or title, you'll want to come up with one that fits the goal. Titles should be a bit more imaginative than just "Beach Party," "The Great Gatsby," or "Pirates in Paradise." Advertising agencies, media companies, and PR firms do an excellent job of creating relevant, catchy titles for events. Spend the time and put some thought into it. Get your team together and brainstorm for five minutes; you will be amazed at what comes out. Tie the look, feel, and goal into a title that clearly identifies the event. For example, we once produced a 1970s dance party in the San Francisco Bay area. The logical name was "The Disco in Frisco." Another event that involved a variety of internationally themed lounges and clubs with an array of themed food, beverages, and entertainment was appropriately named "The Party of the Senses." Lastly, an afterglow event that was to feature a champagne-pouring aerialist and only serve champagne and chocolates was titled "The Bubble Room." The trend today, at most nightclubs and restaurants, is to use one-word names. I think it's pretty hip myself, but sometimes you have to explain the event better with a more descriptive title.

The Blurb

The next part of the proposal should be a paragraph or two at the top explaining the overall feel, or vibe, of the event. The content of that paragraph should hit the highlights of each major component. It should leave the reader with a clear understanding of how the event will look and feel. For example:

"GAME ON"

This evening of high-stakes gaming, wireless trivia, and our big-screen Sports Book featuring championship boxing, NASCAR, and horse racing will provide an exciting kickoff to the annual sales conference. Bring your lucky charm, rabbit's foot, and poker face since the conference kickoff will be sure to challenge both intellect and luck. Be ready to get your "Game On." At the end of the evening, 10:30 p.m., we will host our live auction, using everyone's total winnings from the evening. Be sure to stick around for a mega raffle drawing at the conclusion of the auction.

And then there is this example from an event that was held at the Moon Palace in Mexico; thus I incorporated the name of the hotel into the event title.

"GROOVIN' AT THE MOON"

This year's opening-night event will take place in our ultra-hip nightclub setting, as we create a contemporary lounge environment. Guests will be seated at a combination of tall cocktail tables with barstools and intimate lounge/club-type seating groups, elevated on hotel risers strategically placed throughout the ballroom. Our four-sided brushed metal bar will provide beverage service as well as serving as a central focal point. Inside the backbar will be an elevated platform with costumed dancers. The overall look will be done in all white and brushed metal, with color washes and highlights coming from a variety of overhead moving lights and theatrical LED up-lighting. Our illuminated dance floor and celebrity DJ will surely stoke the fire throughout the evening.

The Body

The body of the proposal should include easy-to-read, clear, and definitive descriptions, with the quantity of all the items being provided. A photo of that exact item or group of items should be included with the description. Do not put a photo of an item and then write "this is not exactly what the item will look like," thus leaving the impression of the old bait-and-switch. I typically spell out all the event components in a line-item menu format that allows the buyer to identify the need-to-have items versus the nice-to-have items.

The Pricing

Back in the olden days, a client would give you a lump sum total for the event. The proposal would come back with a general description of all the items, and have that budget number listed right there at the bottom of the page. Today, buyers are a whole lot more sophisticated. They want to know exactly what they are buying and how much each item costs. They want to ensure that they are not being overcharged for items and that they are getting a fair value for what they've selected. Today's clients expect line-item pricing on proposals. It's a matter of personal preference as to whether you put the price on the same line as the description, or group all of the pricing on one page at the end. I prefer to put the price on the line with the description, so I don't have to flip back and forth to make sure the price fits the description.

In addition to listing all of the items that fit within the proposed budget, it's a good idea to also give the client additional purchase options. Although they may exceed the specified budget, they give the potential client extra choices. You may want to list them at the bottom, after you have totaled all the items and hit the budget number. The buyer may decide it's worth trimming a meatball off the buffet in order to get that extra item you proposed.

The Loose Ends

The last part of the proposal usually contains all of the noncreative, must-have items, such as labor, delivery, shipping, rigging, power, venue charges, and appropriate sales taxes. You also want to define who will be responsible for any on-site or additional charges that you are unaware of at the time of the proposal. Believe me, there are many. It's always best to clearly define who will be responsible for those at the proposal stage versus on-site or after the fact.

Once the proposal has been accepted, the event planning gets rolling. One of the first items you need to tackle is deciding who is coming to the party. Like all facets of event production, this requires serious attention to detail.

The Guest List

You can spend a ton of precious time and your client's money putting together the perfect venue, décor, entertainment, and so on, but if the guest list is messed up, your event can achieve less-than-desirable results. It is a huge embarrassment to invite a subordinate yet overlook the boss or some other VIP who should have received an invitation. That is why, regardless of who created the guest list, I always recommend that another set of eyes check it over carefully. This is to make certain that it neither includes the wrong people nor excludes anyone notable. Sometimes several people will need to look at the list, just to be sure.

Today, people expect documents to be sent electronically, since the computer is where we spend most of our time. This goes for invitations as well, and you can easily send an invite via e-mail or an electronic invitation service provider. This is okay for regular, not-big-deal events, and it is fairly easy to keep track of the RSVPs. However, if you are producing an event that is high profile or is intended to create or signify importance, you should always send a paper invitation via snail mail. Also include a self-addressed RSVP card. It shows considerable more thought and gives the event greater significance.

Once the invitations have been sent, it's time to consider the RSVPs. Who will manage that process? It takes someone who is on top of his or her game, that's for sure. You'd be amazed how often people will RSVP and then not show up. On the flip side, it's just as amazing how many people will not RSVP and then show up. I'm not sure why folks do that. Obviously, they don't realize the financial consequences to the host. The host is buying food, beverages, table décor, transportation, space, and staff based upon the RSVPs.

So, how can you mitigate the no-show factor? The best way to avoid having a bunch of surprise no-shows is to assign the RSVPs to either one person or a group of people—managers, volunteers, or what have you. They should follow up with a personal phone call to each guest on the RSVP list a week before your event. Remind them about the event if they have RSVP'd or ask them why they have not. Sometimes you almost have to give the guests an out, because they may be afraid to tell you no. Try saying, "It's okay if you can't come; we just need to know in advance for planning purposes." If they're not intending to show up, that will usually get them to admit it.

 If you don't follow up on those RSVPs, you could see as much as 40 percent of the guest list not show up. Not only is that expensive, but it also looks horrible to have that many empty seats at your event.

The follow-up on the RSVP is critical. Like I said, you should do it a week before the big day, and then it doesn't hurt to do it again a day or two before the event, just to reconfirm.

Once you get that confirmation and you have a pretty good idea of who is coming, you'll need to think about guest check-in. Ensure that you give out a proper guest credential to attendees when they check in. This will serve as their identification and verify that they are supposed to be there. You'll need an accurate, detailed list of the invited attendees. You'll also need to have some type of staffing or security at the check-in desk, where guests will receive their name badges or credentials. It helps if you have somebody who actually knows the people who are expected to attend.

Do you recall the White House party crashers who showed up at a 2009 state dinner without being on the guest list? They got all the way past security and even shook President Obama's hand. I think that probably qualifies as the biggest party crashing of all time. I can't even begin to imagine how they got past the Secret Service at a formal dinner without being on the invitee list. Don't think that it can't happen. If it can happen at the White House, it can definitely happen at your event. Be diligent.

PRESIDENT OBAMA GREETS PARTY CRASHERS MICHAELE AND TAREQ SALAHI (PHOTO BY ASSOCIATED PRESS)

Putting It All On the Table

Choosing the tables for an event used to be pretty straightforward. There were six- and eight-foot rectangles for buffet lines, round seventy-two-inch tables seating ten or twelve, and round sixty-inch tables seating six or eight—and that was it. But now there are many different sizes and shapes available, including square, oval, and even triangular tables. Figuring out the best ones to use depends first and foremost upon the type of event that you're hosting. Is it going to be a sit-down dinner, a casual barbecue, a club or lounge, or a standing cocktail reception? Are people going to be sitting or standing most of the time? What, exactly, will the tables be used for?

Typically, the six- and eight-foot rectangular banquet tables are for food stations. Round tables are generally used for guest dining. They range in size from cocktail tables that are thirty inches in diameter all the way up to large sit-down tables measuring seventy-two inches. In Mexico, I actually saw the hotel roll out a ninety-six-inch round when they ran out of seventy-two-inch tables. Needless to say, I told them to roll that big boy right back into storage, as I had no linen that would fit on that table. That was a first.

Personally, I like to mix up the seating as much as possible at my events. I don't like looking at a sea of round tables in an event space; it's boring. With today's styles, you have the ability to mix and match a lot of different seating configurations. Restaurants do much the same thing with their booths and dining tables of various shapes and sizes. So, yes, you can mix round tables with square and rectangular tables. You can combine tall tables and bar stools with venue chairs and low cocktail tables. Go ahead. I give you permission!

DARREN'S TIP When I am setting a cocktail reception, I rarely use low cocktail tables with chairs. I want people to mix and mingle—not sit. It is also very awkward to talk to someone while you are standing and he or she is sitting.

ACRYLIC TABLE AND CHAIR SET-UP (PHOTO BY DWJ)

TALL COCKTAIL TABLES WITH BAR STOOLS (PHOTO BY DWJ)

ALTERNATING SQUARE ROUND AND RECTANGULAR TABLES (PHOTO BY DV PIX)

Speaking of chairs, these days they are as varied as the tables. Anytime you are doing an event at a location, take a look at (and take pictures of) all the different types of chairs they have available. Also, be aware that in most cases venues use a separate set of chairs for outside events. Inspect them prior to your event, because those chairs are often severely weathered and not up to standards for a corporate event. If that's the case, you'll need to bring in rental chairs.

Linens

Tablecloths have certainly evolved since I first started in the event production business so many years ago. Back then we had only a handful of different color choices, and they were mainly in one fabric—the old standby, polyester. Then we started to see more colors emerge, along with themed tablecloths and those in lamé—the sparkly metallic fabrics that were en vogue in the eighties. Next up were satin and wild prints, limited only by the imaginations of the designers.

Now, linens are absolutely stunning. There is so much more emphasis on table décor these days, and it's because there are just so many styles and flavors available. There are textured linens, layered linens, and linens that actually light up. It's exciting, but all that excitement comes with a price. Linens have skyrocketed from $10 for each tablecloth to as much as $120 apiece for some of the more elegant options.

Once you've nailed down the style and material for your tablecloths, you have to choose the right size. This is more difficult than you might think, and it's another one of those things that nobody ever teaches you about corporate event production. That's why I made this handy chart–to take out all the guesswork:

TABLE LINEN SIZING/SEATING CHART

Our sizing chart shows the suggested tablecloth sizes for the most commonly used standard-sized tables and tablecloth sizes. All tablecloths are floor length.

Round Tables

Table Size	Linen Size	Seating
30" Round	90" Round	2–4 Guests
36" Round	96" Round	2–4 Guests
42" Round	108" Round	4–5 Guests
48" Round	108" Round	4–6 Guests
54" Round	120" Round	6–8 Guests
60" Round	120" Round	8–10 Guests
66" Round	132" Round	8–10 Guests
72" Round	132" Round	10–12 Guests

Banquet (Rectangular) Tables

6' Banquet	90"x 132" Banquet	6–8 Guests
8' Banquet	90" x 156"Banquet	8–10 Guests

Hi-Top Tables (Airport, Belly Bars, Elbow or Hi-Boys)

24" Round	108" Round	N/A
30" Round	120" Round	N/A
36" Round	120" Round	N/A

Then there are chair covers and napkins, which can be great enhancements to any special event. The napkin and chair cover selections are as varied and vast as the table-cloths. You can find polyester chair covers, spandex, satin, brushed satin, silk, textured, feathered, and just about any crazy fabric you might see on a theatrical costume. Other really cool and hip components include sashes, silk rope tassels, and jeweled bands accented with fresh flowers, beads, feathers, and even grass. Napkins and napkin rings have evolved into showpieces as well; you see the same stylish accents on napkin rings as those used on chair covers. These can be combined to create stunning custom table décor.

As I mentioned previously, if you're thinking of using chair covers, you must take pictures of the chairs you'll be using and show those photos to the linen company supplying the covers. (You might want to take measurements just in case.) Why? Because we're seeing a lot of cases in which venues have chairs with wider-than-normal backs or funky shapes on the back. The standard-sized chair covers do not fit them. It's rather painful to have a 1000 chair covers to put on at a site, only to find out that they don't fit. Trust me—you don't want to discover that problem four hours before your event on a Saturday, when the linen company is closed and you can't get replacements. So be very careful to order covers that will fit the chairs you're using.

(PHOTO BY DV PIX)

SPANDEX LINENS WORK WELL FOR WINDY
LOCATIONS (PHOTO BY DWJ)

CHIVARI CHAIRS WITH CHAIR COVERS (PHOTO BY DWJ)

Table Décor and Floral Centerpieces

Centerpieces on the tables are one of the most important components of any formal or semiformal dinner event. The single most-viewed element of the evening is what is resting in the center of the table, where guests are seated for three to five hours. When deciding how to allocate budget dollars, start with a decent centerpiece first. Then allocate budget dollars for tablecloths, napkins, and chair covers. It is always better to spend more on the centerpiece and less on the linens if you have a tight budget.

One thing I've seen all too often: the train wreck that results when a florist creates centerpieces without knowing what the table linens are going to look like. The next thing you know, there are hot pink tulips and purple irises sitting on top of a yellow-and-orange–striped tablecloth. That has happened too many times to count, especially when people are using loud tropical prints and busy flower arrangements. If that kind of stuff is not well coordinated, it is a recipe for a very ugly table setup. This can cause a lot of tears for somebody. If that table décor ensemble doesn't match, you will definitely hear about it.

DARREN'S TIP My recommendation is to always send a picture of the table linens to the florist, so they can plan their designs around it. Ask them to e-mail shots of their proposed arrangements to you so you can see exactly what is going to be on those tables.

I recall the arrangements that were popular back when I started in the business, and I marvel at how much the designs have changed since then. Back in the seventies and eighties, everything was what we called a "roundy moundy"–meaning it was just a spherical bunch of flowers "usually run-of-the-mill things like daisies, pompoms, and lilies" that had been stuck into a chunk of oasis in a round bowl. Then (thankfully!) things started evolving into taller, more stylish centerpieces, with glass vases and hip containers.

Today, floral designs are absolutely spectacular. For example, now I'm seeing designers mixing multiple shapes and sizes of glass containers on one table using monochromatic florals, which is pretty striking. Also, the designs themselves are more distinctive. They are more "European," meaning that loose flowers are arranged in a way that is very contemporary and fashionable.

Also trending since the early 2000s is the introduction of other mediums to the tabletop décor. One thing that was popular back a few years ago was the frozen centerpiece; ice was everywhere. In fact, it was such a popular party element that I bought an ice manufacturing facility and shipped it to the Bahamas—but that's a whole other book entirely. The craze was to embed items inside the ice, such as flowers, fake jewels, or champagne bottles with the company's name on them. Once we even put Rolex watches inside the ice!

Lately, lots of organic elements, such as chunks of glass or lava, coral, and shells, are being incorporated into the table décor. That gives the tabletop more of an interesting architectural feel than you get from a simple roundy moundy. LED lighting creates an even more spectacular focal point on today's tables. Still, my favorite is flowers. I love elegant flowers on the table, and so do the guests. They're classic. Flowers will never go out of style; they'll just evolve into increasingly cooler and hipper designs.

(PHOTO BY DV PIX)

(PHOTO BY DWJ)

(PHOTO BY DWJ)

Another pre-event planning basic that goes hand in hand with floral is décor. In the industry, the term "décor" applies to anything that can be used to enhance the look or feel of an event space. It includes items such as props, furniture, flowers, linens, plants, and more.

Décor

Décor, or decorations, encompasses the components that you bring into a venue to change, disguise, or enhance the appearance of the site. Décor elements are comprised of themed components: draping, furniture, plants, table coverings, flowers, bars, and food station enhancements, to name just a few. Décor is prioritized as a nice-to-have item when determining a budget. Décor allows the sponsor to really personalize an event, creating an environment specific to that audience. It helps to make a unique event that guests could not experience if they were to visit the same venue on their own.

Décor has changed as much as any other element that we use on a regular basis in the event industry. In the 1980s, appearance became a priority for corporate events, and the term "theme party" was coined. It wasn't your daddy's simple cocktail-party-by-the-pool anymore—the gatherings had to have a theme. Some of the more popular ones were M*A*S*H, Miami Vice, The Great Gatsby, pirates, fifties sock hop, casino, beach, and luau, to name a few. That required themed entertainment, themed food and beverages, and themed decorations. When I first started setting up theme parties, our décor consisted of painted plywood cutouts with colored glitter and a lot of flat, painted facades. Sometimes they were freestanding; others we would lean up against the wall.

Décor has evolved throughout each of the past three decades. Trends changed to be less flashy, bold, and busy; they became three-dimensional, too. What used to be just a plywood cutout of a parrot with some glitter on it transitioned into a giant parrot sculpted from foam. The days of big, prop-filled theme parties gave way to hipper, more stylish environments. Toward that end, the design of today's events has moved from a party atmosphere to an architectural, almost restaurant or lounge-like feel. These days we're doing more events that have casual seating with a relaxed vibe. The seating environments are intimate, with entertainment in the background. This makes it conducive for guests to engage fellow employees, peers, management, and ownership. For example, a "Starbucks-style" setting would be the typical environment that a company would hire us to create. They'd ask us to come in and generate the type of setting in which people could sit and interact, whether they're on social media or face-to-face.

Because of these new settings, the roles of bigger, three-dimensional props and set pieces have changed. They still have a place in events, but they're not the dominant focal point anymore. Now they are used more as background items or accent pieces.

When I am using décor, I try to place it in both the interior areas of the event space and along the perimeter walls. However, at a big gala dinner, you have no choice but to work the perimeter. Décor in the interior part of the space will obstruct the view and sight lines of the stage or video screens. But in parties that have more of a flow, with multiple food stations and strolling or ancillary entertainment, you can create different areas and unique spaces by placing the décor in the middle of the room. I hate seeing an uninterrupted sea of tables. I want guests to wander around and check out what's behind that wall or that building.

GIANTS ICE BAR
(PHOTO BY DV PIX)

LOUNGE SEATING (PHOTO BY DWJ)

AWARDS DINNER (PHOTO BY DWJ)

DISGUISING HOTEL WALLS (PHOTO BY DWJ)

DARREN'S TIP

You have to be careful when placing décor in the interior spaces. Make sure that everything is finished on all sides. If it's not, you will need to use another element to hide the unfinished side.

Over my career, I have owned several event companies with large inventories of décor, both in Florida and the Bahamas. One of the many challenges with owning assets like décor is the ongoing repair and maintenance required to keep the items looking fresh and new. No one wants to see a beat-up prop or décor item with chipped paint. Most damage is incurred when trucking the décor, not at the actual event. Today, companies are much better at using shrink-wrap or packing blankets to ensure minimal damage to the items.

Sometimes I am producing an event at a destination where I do not know the vendor or the décor quality. I always make a point to visit the warehouse of the décor company that I am considering for my event. I can tell very quickly how my décor will look when it gets on-site based on how the warehouse looks. If a warehouse is in a state of disrepair, with piles of stuff everywhere, it is probably not the best choice. Companies that keep clean, organized shops typically own and keep a well-maintained inventory. Whenever possible, go check out your vendors' operations; this will tell you a lot. That holds true with any vendor, especially caterers.

Production

Production is the all-encompassing equipment and staff required to produce entertainment acts, meetings, and a variety of large-scale special events. It includes all the staging, lighting, audio, video, and power necessities. The technology that has evolved in this area over the last three decades is by far the most dramatic of any of the previously-listed event components. Lighting has transitioned from once power-hungry fixtures to extremely efficient LED lighting, giving designers an infinite array of color, moving, and design options. Sound and video have also made giant strides in their quality, clarity, and power the last few decades.

It is extremely important to hire good-quality AV suppliers when you are producing a corporate event. Equipment failures usually spell big trouble, and the entire event could be undermined if the production support falls short. For large events, it is common to have backup equipment in place for the unexpected. Think of your production supplier as the entire utility infrastructure, just like you would for the power, water, telephone, and cable for your home. When those things go down, it typically creates massive issues for those affected; the same applies for your production support.

When choosing a production supplier, you must first understand your needs. Some companies specialize in certain elements, such as just lighting, sound, video, or staging. There are several companies that provide all of these components under one roof. What I mean by you must understand your needs prior to selecting vendors is that not all AV equipment and services are equal, and there are many different levels of service and equipment based on the size and complexity of the event. It is not a one-size-fits-all type of business. Many companies only own the latest and most technologically advanced equipment, which will obviously be the most expensive, while other companies may own older equipment with older technology. The prices will vary quite a bit, so my best advice is to shop around a lot before you select the right partner to ensure you get the right equipment for the job.

I work two different ways. First, I have a list of several smaller to medium-sized AV companies that I work with around the United States. These companies can handle events that have small- to moderate-sized equipment and staff needs. The more the people in attendance, the more the AV needs are. They are very affordable and provide good value.

The second way I work is, if the event is a large one or has very specific, high-end AV needs, I hire a technical director (TD), who actually hires all the needed labor and also contracts all the required equipment providers that are specific or requested for that event. This is where the level of technical sophistication and understanding requires a trained, experienced expert. You will pay the TD a fee, and he or she will handle all of the stuff required to fulfill that job. It makes the production part of the event very painless. It's more expensive, but you don't have to worry about hiring the wrong or inferior suppliers. Remember that the production is the most important element of these event items, just like your utilities at home. Without them, you have no show.

BASIC A/V PACKAGE
(PHOTO BY DWJ)

(PHOTO BY DWJ)

(PHOTO BY DWJ)

Entertainment

Entertainment is one of the most memorable components, probably second only to production. Entertainment has evolved, just like all the other event components have evolved, from just a musical act or stand-up performer to complete theatrical productions with casts of hundreds, interactive dance companies, make-your-own music videos, and a massive list of audience participation acts and services. Audience participation really started becoming more popular in the late 1980s, when audiences wanted more to do than just sit and watch a performance. They wanted to be part of the performance, and thus the evolution started.

To create a killer event, all of these components are important, but these last two, production and entertainment, are the critical ones. People remember killer entertainment, whether they are dancing, watching a performance, or singing karaoke with a live band. They also remember the terrible performances just as much and are more likely to talk about them than the good ones. People today expect good–no, they expect *great* performances. They will not remember the linens, the flowers, the food, or the color of the room, but they always remember the entertainment, good or bad.

There are two keys to having good entertainment at your event. First, I highly recommend finding a great talent agent. They are experts in entertainment and can help you determine your needs and distill the vast array of options. They can provide access to live performances to see the act before you book it, and they can also provide marketing material of their stable of acts to preview. Talent agents charge a fee, usually 20 percent on top of the act, but sometimes it's actually paid by the act for the booking and marketing services the agent provides. Talent agents also will be on-site during your event to ensure all the details are covered, such as parking, hotel rooms, meals, green rooms, and a bunch of other necessary evils.

SOLO PIANIST (PHOTO BY DWJ)

DARREN WITH MAIN ACT ON BIG OUTDOOR STAGE (PHOTO BY KMJ)

The second most critical element to providing killer entertainment is having killer production support to ensure your act sounds and looks the very best it can. That means a high-quality sound system and a professional lighting system with an audio and lighting designer. These elements vary greatly depending on the price and popularity of the act. Remember, the more popular the act, the more costly the production rider. Use quality talent agents and production suppliers; you'll never go wrong or look bad.

The last part of pre-event planning is determining how and when everything is going to come together. The event producer must deal with the logistics of getting all of the vendors into the site and set up, as well as getting all of them packed up and out of the site at the end. With the appropriate planning and forethought, this process can be well-organized and seamless.

Juggling the Logistics

One of your many jobs as an event producer is determining the load-in schedule. When I say "schedule," I'm talking about creating a workable timetable for the load-in process prior to your event. Loading in involves everything that each vendor needs to bring into and set up at the venue. It is crucial that you create such a schedule, detailing what time every vendor is coming in, how long it will take them to offload their truck and pull the truck away from the loading area, and how long it will take them to set up their particular element(s). You're going to have a whole bunch of different vendors coming and going with equipment and décor, and all kinds of logistics moving into that specific venue in a short period of time. If you want that process to go smoothly (and I know you do!), you're going to have to do some serious advance planning.

For example, if the event producer prepares a good load-in schedule, the florist will be able to bring the flowers in and place them directly on the tables with no hassles. You don't want the florist to bring the flowers in only to discover that the linens are not down. Then they will have to figure out where to place the flowers until the linens go down. In the meantime, the flowers will get knocked around by carts and staff, and probably be in the way of somebody else trying to do a different job.

DARREN'S TIP

Building an event is no different than building a house. You don't want your roof trusses delivered before your slab has even been poured. You do not want your kitchen cabinets delivered when workers are still busy framing the house. Keep that analogy in mind as you plan how all of your event elements will come together.

(PHOTO BY DWJ)

(PHOTO BY DV PIX)

Not only that, but many of your vendors will be charging you based on equipment rental and labor. Labor is based on how long it takes the vendor to get the item delivered, installed, set up, and tested. If you have an eight-man crew waiting to install their lighting and they have to wait two, three, or four hours, you can bet they are charging you for the wait time. That's a common example of bad planning. Do not have all of your vendors arrive at the same time simply because that is the time you have access to the room. Schedule based on their job functions.

REPEAT AFTER ME: TIME IS MONEY

Typically, the order of the event load-in is:

1. Anything that's going to be hung from the ceiling, whether it's sound, lighting, videos, or decorations
2. Staging
3. Sound, lighting, large décor and any other big features on the floor
4. Seating (tables and chairs)
5. Linens and flowers
6. Entertainment
7. Food and beverage

The reverse happens after the close of the event. Typically, it's "first in, last out" (or FILO). Let's say the event ends at midnight. What you don't want is your sound and light company showing up at 12:01 expecting to drop the trusses with the sound and lighting. There are still decorations, tables, a stage, catering supplies, and band equipment lying around. Where are they going to go? Simultaneous things can be going on if they are related to items that are on the ground, but sound and light people can't do much until the room is clear. Consequently, you might schedule them to arrive a few hours after the first crew is due to arrive.

Scheduling is an essential element in producing an event correctly, efficiently, and within budget. Neglect it at your peril.

(PHOTO BY DV PIX)

"The more you sweat in peace, the less you bleed in war!"

– The United States Marine Corps

Remember...

- Keep the language in your proposal simple and straightforward.
- Include pictures of the actual items your client will receive.
- Create imaginative (yet meaningful!) event titles and descriptions that communicate exactly what the event is all about.
- Give line-item pricing.
- Always offer add-ons even if they exceed the budget.
- Define who will be responsible for any unforeseen charges that might crop up.
- Check and double-check the guest list to make sure it's correct.
- Follow up with everyone on the RSVP list at least once, but preferably twice, before the event.
- Establish a fail-safe check-in and credential system at the door.
- Don't be afraid to mix and match different sizes, shapes, and styles of tables.
- If you think you might want to use chair covers, be sure to take photographs of the venue's chairs during your site inspection to ensure the chair cover fits the chair. If you are not sure the photo shows everything clearly, measure the width of the back just in case.
- Send your florist a picture of your linen choices, so he or she can coordinate the tabletop décor.
- Trends have shifted from big and bold décor elements to stylish and lounge-type environments more conducive for conversation.
- Make sure décor and centerpieces don't block anyone's view of the stage or video screens.
- Check out the cleanliness and order of your vendors' facilities and warehouses for clues to how the equipment and products will look at your event.
- A carefully prepared load-in/load-out schedule is critical to your event's success.

Chapter 5

Event Safety Planning

"I get by with a little help from my friends"
— *John Lennon and Paul McCartney*

E vent safety planning has become a vital component in the planning stages of all events. All too often you hear of tragic accidents that occur at events. They can be weather related, or result from stages being not properly secured, boats being overloaded, or indoor pyro causing fires and killing dozens of people. Because of these possibilities, every aspect of your event should go through a thorough review and scrutiny. You should ensure that all vendors are using the highest quality and standards in their products and services. You never want to use the low bidder in something as important as safety issues. There may be hidden reasons they are the low bidder. Due to the increase in incidents that have occurred over the years, municipalities are now holding event producers to much higher standards. They are ensuring that proper safety measures are in place prior to issuing necessary permits.

Permits: Who Needs 'Em?

Obtaining permits has become a routine function in the event production world today. In just about every instance, we have to submit a CAD drawing to the venue, which in turn submits that plan to the fire department for approval. While this is not technically a "permit," you will need the fire marshal's endorsement stating that you are adhering to all fire and safety measures. These measures would include proper egress, no flammable storage in the room, no obstructed sprinkler heads, and proper aisle widths. Permits are not free; you'll have to budget money and time for securing them. But you might as well get used to it; this approval is something you'll need to have on hand in order to secure various other items.

Let's start with tents. When you hire a company to erect a tent, you will usually have to procure a permit from your local municipality. A few places don't require it, but most locations do—especially here in my home state of Florida. Sometimes the tent company will get the permit for you; others will want you to get it yourself. So you always need to ask the tent company who is responsible for procuring the permit. Tent permits can cost anywhere from $75 to $300 depending on the municipality in which you're operating and can take several weeks for approval.

Permits are often required for any type of outdoor event—especially if you're holding it in a public space like a state or city park. Some municipalities even require them for private spaces. Usually the permit application has to show a drawing of all of the components of the event. This includes where the stage is, if there will be emergency services on-site, how emergency service vehicles will get in and out of the site, if there's proper egress…you know the drill. It's just like holding an event in a hotel ballroom or any other indoor venue. You have to show all of that stuff and also verify that you have fire marshal approval when you're requesting an outdoor event permit.

Recently, I have been required to get a permit for outdoor music—even if it's only a DJ. I recently produced a tailgating event for a college football bowl game, and much to my surprise, the city required this permit. Apparently this requirement was created because football games and other outdoor events often have the music playing super loud. The city had no real guidelines or ordinances that could make the event people turn the music down. So the city council created a permit that includes very specific guidelines on how loud (in decibels) you can play the music. If you violate those guidelines, they will revoke your permit and shut your event down. Anytime you're going to produce an outdoor event, be sure to check with the municipality and the venue to find out whether or not any type of music permits are going to be required.

Other things that you definitely have to procure permits for are indoor and outdoor fireworks, pyrotechnics, or laser shows. Those usually require that the fire marshal provide a crew on-site in case of any emergency mishaps. Frequently you have to get a city permit and a fire permit for any type of pyrotechnics.

Events in Other Countries: Important items that you need to be aware of whenever you are producing an event outside of the United States are work permits and staff permits. In just about any country outside the United States, all of your staff is going to be required to apply for work permits. They basically tell the host country's immigration agency that you are there for a specific period of time, doing a specific job, and then you are leaving.

A lot of times you can fly under the radar without those permits, and it will not be an issue. But it's a very unpleasant feeling when immigration officials show up at your venue and ask to see your permits. If your staff does not have those permits, then you are kindly escorted to the airport and put on the next flight out of there. You do not want to experience that. It is always better to follow those countries' guidelines and apply for the permits. They are not cheap; sometimes they can run in excess of $300 to $500 per permit. Apply for the permits at least six or eight weeks before you're going out of the country, so you have them in hand. Contact the host country's immigration bureau to inquire about their rules and regulations. Just know that whenever a permit is required, the more time you give the issuing body, the easier it will be to obtain.

Although all of the permits that I have discussed are necessary and important, the overriding issues that concern event safety planning ultimately lie with the fire marshal.

Working with the Fire Marshal

Everyone probably remembers Jim Carrey's iconic character Fire Marshall Bill, from the television show *In Living Color*. Bill, who was supposed to be ensuring fire safety, caught himself on fire. He was a hilarious character.

But in the real world of corporate event production, fire marshals are no joke. They are a necessary result of the many unfortunate incidents and accidents at events in the past. Today, fire marshal rules and regulations are much stricter than ever before. Most hotels, venues, public spaces, and arenas now have to submit their events to the fire marshal for prior approval. Without that approval, the event isn't going to happen.

In some cases, you'll submit the required paperwork directly to the fire marshal, but most often you'll prepare the documents and give them to the venue. Your contact will then submit the information to the fire marshal on your behalf. The first thing you have to provide is a CAD drawing. Complying with fire safety codes is a key reason event producers must have a CAD. This is the computer-aided drawing that we discussed in Chapter 3, "Selecting and Inspecting Your Venue." It shows the placement of all of the equipment and tables, the width of the aisles, and the location of all the exit doors, among other things.

DARREN'S TIP — Although it is not an official, universal policy, there is a rule of thumb stating that one emergency exit is required for every one hundred people. I follow that formula until I learn otherwise.

Once you have your CAD done, you need to identify all of the items on the drawing. If you're using any kind of coverings around the room or walls, you have to be sure that the exit signs, fire hoses, and strobes are not covered up. You also have to show that there is no cabling going across the egress doors, that nothing will interfere with the fire hoses or the fire sprinklers that are in the ceilings, and that all of the items being placed in the event space are fire-retardant or fireproof.

On many occasions, I have watched a fire marshal go into a room and actually light something on fire to see whether or not it will burn. If it burns, he will make you take it out of the room right that second. Most of the time, the fire marshal will just want to see your flame-retardant or fireproofing certificates for all the fabrics, structures, or décor items in the room. You can get those certificates from the supplier that's providing those goods for you. So keep that in mind when you're ordering, and request them up front.

Another item that I touched on previously is *egress*. Egress is essentially how people will get out of the room in case of an emergency. You have to make sure that those exit doors are not blocked, that there are no trip hazards, and that there's proper emergency lighting to illuminate those doors.

When you have big productions, you may be covering a lot of doors. When you are permitted to cover an exit door, make sure the emergency exit sign for that door is always covered. Why? Because if you don't cover the sign and the power goes off, the emergency lighting for that exit door will come on. People will run to that exit only to find it blocked. So in the event that you do get approval to block a door, just make sure that you also cover the signage. Then nobody will see it as a potential exit in case of an emergency.

Finally, fire marshals have very strict guidelines regarding parking for trucks and employees. You must ensure that fire, police, and emergency medical vehicles have easy access in and out of the space. You also have to make sure that the fire hydrants are not blocked.

Just know that fire marshals have the ultimate authority. Do not think you can work around what the fire marshal says. If you have not complied with their requests, they will absolutely shut your event down. This will happen whether it is one minute before the doors open or right in the middle of the event. And they do not care one bit if a VIP is in attendance, be it Brad Pitt, Tim Tebow, or the president of the United States. Conduct your planning with that truth in mind. And work closely with local fire authorities in advance, so there are no big surprises on Event Day.

Once the fire marshal has signed off on your event, your next concerns will apply to the event itself. During large events, security and emergency services personnel may be required.

Play it Safe

When you're producing a large event, it will often be necessary to hire security and emergency services personnel to be on-site. With large crowds, there is always the potential for someone to twist an ankle, fall down stairs, run into a pole, or make some other not-so-smooth move. It's always a good practice to have paramedics nearby anytime you have a large event, just in case you have an accident. Security helps with crowd control and event admission. If money is changing hands or any other type of financial transactions are going on, having visible security on-site helps deter theft or stupid decisions. They can also swiftly deal with any issue that does occur.

IMPORTANCE OF HAVING GOOD INSURANCE: DUDE JUGGLING CHAINSAWS (PHOTO BY DWJ)

Most corporate events don't require uniformed police on-site. That is geared more toward public events, where you have a large gathering of people that you don't know. Having police at the entrance to such an event can be a deterrent to anybody who may have bad intentions. If somebody gets out of hand, you have the ability to remove him or her quickly.

In contrast, if you're hosting an exclusive corporate event, typically you'll hire a private security force that is much less conspicuous. Having a uniformed deputy with a gun and a badge at the door to your swanky cocktail reception can send the wrong message. Usually you will have a plainclothes security staff on-site that has access to local emergency services. Their main job, however, is to make sure that only invited guests are admitted, that people are displaying the right credentials, and that the media doesn't get into the event without permission. If there is a problem with a wacko, a crazy mother-in-law, or a protester, they can remove the offender(s) in a quiet, effective manner, to be dealt with off-site.

As the producer of the event, it's your responsibility to contract those services. I estimate that these days, a large portion of all events have security on-site. This started changing in the nineties and really took off after 9/11. Before that, we rarely had security guards at corporate events, unless we had a dignitary there. We never had Occupy Wall Street people or homeless people protesting outside. We never had PETA outside picketing because there was a guy at our event with a parrot on his shoulder taking pictures with the attendees. We never had people suing because they fell and twisted their ankle and blamed the client or the venue. We never had people taking weapons into an event. Now there are a gazillion reasons why we usually have security at the event.

I vividly remember when the financial crisis started unfolding in 2008 and AIG got busted in Burbank for having lavish events. The story broke about them spending big money on corporate events and then receiving government bailout money. Instantly that created a media feeding frenzy. Every local media outlet began stalking the hotels, looking for evidence of a financial institution having a party. They would scan the reader boards outside the venues to see who was having an event. They would quiz the hotel bartenders or banquet captains for inside information on who was having events at their facility. Suddenly everybody and their brother with a flip phone or camera was taking pictures of corporate events and posting them on the Internet. It was an absolute media delirium, and Corporate America went into total vapor lock. They just shut it down.

So now people are very paranoid about media scrutiny. Security helps minimize that fear by making sure your client's privacy is protected. It's worth the expense for that peace of mind. Dealing with all safety concerns—including such safety issues as extra vigilance at nontypical venues—gives the event producer peace of mind.

Safety Due Diligence

Anytime you're producing an event at a place that is not a typical event venue—warehouse, museum, park, stadium, racetrack, airplane hangar, and so on—you need to keep a keen eye out for any potential safety hazards or risks. You'll do this during your initial site inspection, and also before and during the event. Check for loose electrical sockets in the wall and stair railings that look shaky or flimsy. Steep staircases are a common hazard. People have a tendency to slip coming down them if they're not at the proper grade. Pay careful attention to balconies: They may have excessively low rails or other areas where people could easily accidentally fall off. Be on the lookout for uneven pavement, potholes, or holes in lawns that someone might step in and trip.

Also, you'll want to make sure that the exit doors are not locked or chained and that no equipment is parked in front of them. One frequent problem is exit doors that are chained on the inside to prevent people coming in from the outside. You always want to deal with those types of issues, even though the fire marshal may not have inspected the venue—yet. Take care of that well in advance.

There are so many potential hazards at these venues that can cause an accident, injury, or worse. It is your responsibility to make sure that the venue and the event meet all of the necessary safety requirements. Also, ensure that you have quick access to emergency personnel in case something does go wrong, despite your best efforts.

Our last safety consideration is weather. Mother Nature is fickle and unpredictable; the best protection against a weather-related calamity is planning. The safety of your client and guests is of the utmost importance when planning outdoor events.

Weather, Again

The final word in event safety is reserved for our old nemesis, the weather. If you are producing an outdoor event and inclement weather is approaching, be prepared to make a decision. Whether it's wind, hail, lightning, flooding, or any combination thereof, it is your responsibility to determine if the situation could be dangerous to your guests, then proceed accordingly. Don't be afraid to make that decision.

A tragic example of a weather hazard happened at the Indiana State Fair in 2011, when a storm came up at an outdoor concert featuring the band Sugarland. Right before the band was set to take the stage, the wind suddenly became ferocious. It flipped the roof of the stage over, killing seven and injuring dozens more. Had the band been performing when it happened, they could also have been among the fatalities.

There is no excuse for that happening. Those storms don't just sneak up on people. When big black clouds roll in like that, you have to be the one to sound the alarm. Get everybody to a safe location, whether it's in buses or shelters or what have you. It is your responsibility, as the producer, to make those calls.

Sometimes the storms go away, but you need to err on the side of caution. Make a weather call whenever there is a potential for injury or risk—especially in the spring and summer. Thunderstorms at those times can generate winds in excess of seventy miles per hour. Those winds will rip tents to shreds, flip stages over, and do damage that you can't imagine—all in the blink of an eye. Be diligent. Keep your eyes to the skies, and make that call when the situation warrants.

(PHOTO BY PHOTODISC®)

Remember...

- Find out the permitting rules of the municipality in which you are operating.
- Request permits well in advance of the event to avoid disappointment.
- When ordering tents, find out if you or the tent company will be securing the appropriate permits.
- Don't take chances with foreign work permits.
- Find out the fire marshal's requirements are for your venue as early in the planning process as possible.
- When ordering goods, ask the supplier for the fire-retardant and fireproofing certificates whenever relevant.
- Cover the emergency exit signs over every blocked exit door.
- Pay attention to parking to make sure no hydrants are blocked and that there is sufficient passage for emergency vehicles.
- Hire security and medical personnel for any large event.
- If you think you need security for a private event, bring in plainclothes officers.
- Remember to conduct your safety due diligence before and during every event.
- Watch the skies and don't be afraid to make a weather call. You're responsible for keeping everyone safe from the storm.

Chapter 6

Food and Drink 101

"It ain't what you don't know that gets you into trouble. It's what you know for sure that just ain't so."

— Mark Twain

If you have produced any type of event, whether it is social, corporate, or public, then you know that catering (food and beverage) could be an entire book by itself. I'm just going to pass on a few of the things that I've learned in the process of hiring catering professionals—those from hotels and other venues, as well as outside independent catering companies.

Menu Planning

Two elements are vital for a killer event—good food and good music. Right now we're going to talk about the food. There are several questions you should ask yourself when beginning the menu-planning part of the process. Here are the three most important:

What do you serve?

How do you serve it?

How much do you serve?

What Do You Serve?

The answer to this question is an essential component of the event goal. This is generally driven by five important facts:

- First and foremost, what is the size of your budget?
- Second, who are your attendees?
- What is the goal or type of event you are having?
- What is the venue or location?
- What is the timing of your event?

It seems as though instead of creating an answer, we have created five more questions. In order to select the proper menu, you really do need to address all of these questions. Sometimes it is very obvious; for instance, if you are putting on a rodeo, you won't be having stir-fry and pasta stations. Instead, you'll be providing some form of grill and BBQ selections.

I have learned from many years of experience not to waste time on menu planning until a real food budget is set. Then, if you have $100 per person, you can get creative and develop a unique menu. If you have $10 per person, then there are a lot fewer options. Prior to putting yourself and your caterer through unnecessary exercises, get the budget.

The next determining factor is your guests. If they are well-traveled foodies, you will want to present something that is of the highest possible quality. The budget may limit the types of food you can offer, but only provide the absolute best items for the money. If the guests are less sophisticated or not very well traveled, simpler, more recognizable foods may be more appropriate. If they are from an international destination or under twenty-one years old, then chicken fingers and macaroni and cheese may be the best options. Always find out who the guests are going to be prior to menu planning.

TABLE LADY (PHOTO BY DWJ)

The goal or the type of event is another key factor in determining what you serve. If it is a two-hour reception and mingling is important, do not serve food that requires a fork and knife to cut. Provide bite-sized food items that can be served on small plates; these are easiest to mix and mingle with. If the goal of the event is to recognize or reward, then a sit-down dinner is more appropriate. If the meal is to be served (a plated dinner), then you need to take into consideration any dietary needs of guests. You also need to ensure that your food service provider is capable of properly executing this type of event with trained service staff.

The venue plays an important role in the selection of the menu. Outdoor spaces usually allow for BBQ smokers, grill stations, and more casual food selections. That does not mean you cannot execute a five-course plated dinner under the stars. You can with the proper caterer. Indoor spaces, such as museums, typically work best with smaller food stations and bite-sized portions, due to limited space and seating. You want to ensure that your food selection matches the venue and flows nicely together.

The last item in the selection process is timing. Depending on the time of day that your event is scheduled, you need to have appropriate food selections and portions. I think this one item gets mishandled more than any other.

DARREN'S TIP

If your event is going to cover a typical meal period, then plan on serving food items and portions that will accommodate a meal for each guest. If you only provide a crudité platter for an event held from 6 to 9 p.m., then you are going to have a lot of hungry, unhappy guests. If the budget doesn't allow for heavier food, then change the time.

How Do You Serve It?

There are basically three ways that you can serve a food function. The first method is *butler-passed*. Uniformed food service staff move through the crowd with platters of bite-sized appetizers and napkins, offering them to each guest. This is a very effective and upscale way to present appetizers or horsd'oeuvres. However, it's not the most effective way to serve a lot of people a lot of food.

The second way to serve is to create a *buffet* (food stations). Guests go to the food and select the items they would like. I recommend using food service personnel to serve the food, or at least the protein, versus allowing the guests to serve themselves. This accomplishes two things: portion control and a professional appearance. When presenting food this way, I prefer using multiple smaller food stations, rather than one gigantic buffet. At the smaller food stations, you can incorporate some type of action, such as a chef-attended station where food is either cut or cooked in front of you. It provides for a much more upscale presentation.

REALLY HIP ICE SUSHI BAR (PHOTO BY DWJ)

(PHOTO BY DWJ)

The third way to present the food is a *plated* or *served meal*. This is a more formal presentation; it requires the food service provider to have trained and plentiful staff in order to properly execute this style of service. The key word is *properly*. It is recommended for events where scheduling is a key concern. Plated meals allow for synchronized timing when multiple speakers, awards, and entertainment are scheduled throughout the evening or between courses. This type of service provides for a much smoother and more timely event itinerary and show flow. Surprisingly, at hotels a plated service is less expensive than providing food stations. This is because the hotel already has the staff on payroll, and they can control their food costs much more effectively with a plated meal than with a buffet. An off-premise caterer may have to charge more for a plated meal because they have to hire more servers in order to execute the food service. There are two ways of providing a plated meal; the most common style is English service, where the servers present a preportioned plate in front of each guest. The second and more upscale way is to provide French service, where the server presents platters of food and serves the guest from the platter. This takes a lot of personnel and a caterer who really knows what he or she is doing.

I suppose you can say that there are four ways to serve, because using all three of these serving techniques together is extremely effective. You can have tray-passed appetizers, a plated second and main course, and then provide dessert stations where guests can create their own concoction, be it sundaes, smoothies, chef-presented bananas Foster, or cherries jubilee.

DARREN'S TIP Try to match the food type and presentation style to the event goal. If time is tight, such as at a luncheon, you may consider presetting the first course, where the food is already on the table prior to guests coming. If time is not critical, I do not recommend presetting a first course.

How Much Do You Serve?

Once you have decided on how you will be serving the food, you need to determine how much to order. When you are working with a hotel or caterer, they will usually require a guaranteed guest count three to five days prior to your event. It is customary for them to have food for an additional 5 percent over and above what you guarantee. Once you are inside the guarantee time frame, you can increase the count slightly, but you cannot decrease it since all the food has already been procured. How much you order will greatly depend on the timing of the event, as I indicated previously. If you are having the event over a meal period, regardless of how you are serving it, get ready to serve a substantial quantity of food. When providing any type of food station that has shrimp, crab, or lobster, be prepared to get hammered. People love those items and will eat much more of it than you expect.

The Caterer

Now that you have figured out the what, the how, and the how much, the next step is to select a qualified food service provider. If you are contracted with a hotel, you will have no choice. If you are producing an event at a different location, follow the advice discussed next.

First and foremost, get references. Whether you're using venue catering or an independent catering company, check their references before you engage them with any type of food and beverage contract. Find out about the company, either by researching online or by talking to other people who have hired them. Ask about the quality of their food, how the service was, if they were on time, and if they were dependable. Was the hot food hot and the cold food cold? How were the flavor profiles and portions? You need to know all of these things. It is great to arm yourself with this information prior to meeting with the caterer. If there were some issues from a previous event, you can bring it up and talk about it during your interview or at the proposal stage. References are very important—and revealing—things to have.

Once you have narrowed down your caterer options, you need to go through the process of identifying the food and beverages that your client's taste and budget allow.

My next recommendation is to set up a tasting. A tasting consists of nothing more than sitting down with the caterer and having him or her serve you the exact meal (or various meal options) that would be served to the guests at your event.

At the tasting, watch out for portion size. Are the portions you are being served the same size your guests can expect to receive? A lot of times in a tasting setting, the caterer will give you a larger portion because he or she is only cooking for one or two, versus fixing those items for 500 or a 1,000. So, buyer beware. You'll want to reconfirm with the catering company that this is the exact portion size your guests will be getting.

Portions are especially important when you are buying a certain amount or buying by the piece count. You can find yourself out of food very quickly by not purchasing the right amount. Make sure you have a guarantee on the number of pieces you are purchasing, as well as the portion size. If it's supposed to be a four-ounce lobster tail, five shrimp per person, or a six-ounce filet, you want to get that in writing. When it comes time for your event and you expect to get a six-ounce filet, you don't want to be served a three-ounce filet. That stuff does happen. Don't let it happen to you and your clients.

The same goes for the food's appearance. Sometimes the food is more attractive at a tasting. The caterer can spend more time creating a masterpiece when he or she has only to make a couple of plates. Confirm that the presentation you're seeing at the tasting is the same thing that your guests will be seeing at your event.

DARREN'S TIP

Take pictures of the plates when you do the tasting. That way, you'll have a record of the dishes, just in case. How big was that pile of mashed potatoes? What was the garnish on the plate? Exactly how many shrimp were there? This helps ensure that the caterer knows you expect to see the same quality and presentation at your event.

Whenever you're dealing with off-premise caterers, it is always smart to visit their commissary and see where they prepare their food. Most clean places are more than eager to show you their commissary and give you a tour of their back-of-the-house operation. You'll get a good idea of how they run their business. It's an educational thing. You will feel more comfortable knowing that the back-of-the-house is clean, and it will give you confidence that they're probably going to do a good job for you.

You'll also want to discuss staffing, and get that down on paper, too. How many staff are they going to provide for your event? How many bartenders will there be? How many servers are there going to be per table? You want to make sure that if you're having a sit-down dinner, you don't have one server trying to cover four tables. When that happens, the first table gets theirs, and thirty minutes later, the last person is being served. You usually want to have one server for every two tables; one per table is optimum. Then everybody can get their food at close to the same time.

If you're having food stations or buffets, how many people are going to be working at those? How many will be clearing tables? If you're having food stations at a cocktail party, you sure don't want to have dirty dishes piling up on tables or tray jacks. You want to be certain there will be adequate staff to address those issues. That is essential information to have on the front end.

Beverages

Rule number one when it comes to providing food and beverage service for an event is: get a drink in the guest's hand as soon as he or she arrives. Even if you just serve sparkling water or trayed-up beer or wine, it immediately relaxes the person. It also gives guests something to do with their hands until they find a person to mingle with. People hate waiting in lines when they first get there—or anytime, really. That is why I highly recommend providing some type of trayed-up drinks that servers can offer guests as they walk in.

When it comes to purchasing alcoholic beverages for your event, you can do it one of three ways:

- Purchase beverages on a per person basis.
- Purchase on a consumption basis.
- Provide a cash bar (where guests pay for beverages themselves).

If you have heavy drinkers, you may choose to pay an hourly price. It may cost you more, but you will know exactly how much you are going to pay. There will be no surprises, unless you go overtime. I think the most economical way to purchase any type of beverage is on a consumption basis. But when you do that, you have to be diligent in your reconciliation at the close of the event. You have to know how many bottles the caterer or the venue started with, and at the end of the night, you count the empty bottles that were consumed. It's very easy to pad that number, so stay vigilant. Keeping those venues and vendors on their toes is your job.

The next part of the bar purchase program is to determine what kind of bar you want to have. Generally you have two choices: a premium bar or a standard (well brand) bar. The premium bar usually includes top-shelf liquors, such as Grey Goose, Johnny Walker Black, Makers Mark bourbon, Crown Royal, and so on. The standard bar may have less expensive brands. No matter what you select when contracting, always get the caterer to provide you with a list. That does two things: allows you to change any items prior to the event, and ensures that no inferior substitutions are provided.

The cash bar can be either a standard bar or a premium bar, and the decision is usually based on who the attendees are. If it's a more sophisticated and well-traveled group, you probably would want to select the premium bar. If it's a less sophisticated or lower income group, you would probably select the standard bar. Here, again, it's important to understand who your attendees are. After all, you don't want to shock your guests with $9 cocktails if they are hourly wage earners.

As a responsible event producer, you want to make sure that your attendees are not being overserved at the event. If you see that somebody has been overserved, you'll want to deal with him or her promptly. You can suggest that the person not have anything more to drink, and let the bar managers and bartenders know to cut the person off from further alcohol consumption. You must then see to it that the intoxicated person is escorted to his or her room or otherwise dealt with safely and appropriately.

(PHOTO BY DV PIX)

(PHOTO BY DV PIX)

DANCERS IN ICE BAR
(PHOTO BY DWJ)

Remember...

- The two most important components of an event are good food and good music.
- Get current references every time.
- Have a tasting of the meal, exactly as the caterer intends to serve it to your guests.
- Make sure the portion sizes are what your guests can expect.
- For future reference, take pictures of each dish as it is presented to you for tasting.
- Ask for a tour of the kitchen area and the back of the house.
- Find out how much staff the caterer is planning to bring. Is it enough to give your guests excellent service?
- Watch out for padded beverage costs, especially when paying on a consumption basis.
- Prevent overconsumption of alcohol and deal swiftly with any that does occur.
- Get the liquor list in writing to ensure that inferior substitutions are not used.
- Get some type of beverage into the guests' hands as soon as possible.

Chapter 7

When Disaster Strikes

"Problems are only opportunities in work clothes."
— Henry J. Kaiser

During thirty years of producing live events, I have experienced my fair share of things that went wrong. Some could have been avoided; others could not. Ironically, the lack of a contingency plan is exactly how I got started in this business; an event completely imploded, and I happened to be right in the front row.

I think the ability to cope with or avoid a disaster at a live event is at the very core of success in this field. This applies whether you're producing events for your company or you're in business for yourself as an event producer. There is one absolute fact: it's not a matter of if you will face a disaster—it's *when* you will face a disaster.

Once Upon a Time

In the summer of 1982, at the wise old age of twenty-one, I had just been honorably discharged from the United States Marine Corps after serving a four-year stint as a jet mechanic. I relocated to sunny Fort Lauderdale, Florida, where I obtained gainful employment as a bartender at Chuck's Steakhouse.

After working at Chuck's for a couple of months, I came to know my regular customers, people who would come in and eat at the bar on a weekly basis. One of them

UNITED STATES MARINE DARREN W. JOHNSON 1978

was a woman named Janelle. She appreciated my company, and needless to say, I appreciated her generous tips. Janelle was in the event and entertainment business, and she really looked the part. She sported a poufy Charlie's Angels hairdo, was a sharp dresser, and was dripping with diamonds. Did I mention she was a good tipper?

One evening, Janelle came in for dinner at the bar and asked me if I knew how to drive a twenty-four-foot box truck. I told her, "Of course I do; I'm a Marine." She then offered me $100 to drive a truck with some props in it across the state, from Fort Lauderdale to an event she was producing at the Marco Beach Marriott. I would then help set it up, take it down when the event was over, and bring it back to Fort Lauderdale that same night. Back then, one hundred bucks was equivalent to about three hundred today. For a guy making $2.25 per hour and $40 a day in tips, it was big money. I didn't hesitate for one second to say yes.

The day arrived for me to pick up the truck, get it loaded, and drive it to the hotel. The Marco Beach Marriott sits on an expanse of stunning, sugar-white-sand beach and consists of two tall connected towers. One side faces east, toward the Everglades, and the other faces west, toward the Gulf of Mexico. It's the perfect party location, especially as the sun goes down over the Gulf each evening. It provides a free, spectacular sunset celebration. But on this particular day—unbeknownst to us: the event planner, the hotel staff, and the client hosting the event—a bank of giant black clouds had been building throughout the afternoon on the Everglades (east) side of the building. The two tall hotel towers completely blocked our view of the approaching storm.

It was almost time for the event to start. The band was set up and doing its sound check, the hotel bartenders were in place, all the linens and centerpieces were down, and all the food was on the buffets. The band began playing as the guests stepped out into the tropical paradise, filling in around the pool and event space. By all appearances, it was going to be a great party. But about ten minutes after the party started, a wall of ginormous black clouds appeared directly overhead and unleashed a thunderstorm of unimaginable fury. I mean, it was the whole enchilada: torrential rain, forty-mile-per-hour winds, booming thunder, and cracking lightning. The wind was blowing so hard that the tables were flipping over, even the ones with food on them. It happened so quickly that nothing could be saved. Welcome to summertime in Florida, baby!

The obvious question to me was why no one had bothered to check the weather forecast, or at least look out the other side of the hotel to see what was forming on the horizon. Storms of that size usually give advance notice of their intensity and path. You have at least enough forewarning to move the food, bars, band, and some décor inside before all hell breaks loose.

Approximately ten minutes into the storm, the hotel agent and the client came to talk to my coworker and me. They wanted to know if we could possibly move all of the décor, lighting, and plants inside to another location. This was where youth, Marine-

"The Marines have landed, and the situation is well in hand."

– Richard Harding Davis, war correspondent

instilled invincibility, and plain stupidity converged to formulate the answer that came from my mouth: "Sure. We'll go get the stuff. No problem."

When I said we could, I did not think they meant right then, in the teeth of the storm. As we loaded all the rain-drenched décor and plants into the truck, the storm hammered us with sheets of pouring rain, gusting wind, booming thunder, and popping lightning. We were soaked to the bone in seconds, and of course we had no jackets, raincoats, or dry clothes to change into. Looking back at it now, some thirty years later, there is no way I would have allowed my employees to go out in a storm that violent.

They told us the hotel needed forty-five minutes to replenish the food that was lost in the rain and to reset the party inside the empty exhibit hall. We completed the move in an hour's time, well ahead of the hotel being ready with fresh food and a reset room—not counting the band getting their equipment dry and working. It must have been a hotel sales guy who said that it would only take forty-five minutes. As it turned out, that didn't happen. Neither that hotel nor any other would be able to take an absolutely bare room and completely set it up with tables, chairs, stage, dance floor, linens, complete bar, and replacement food in only forty-five minutes.

Still, the group ended up having a great event, and a good time was had by all. The hotel and client couldn't thank us enough for going the extra mile to make it happen. The next morning, we headed back to Fort Lauderdale, unloaded the décor, returned the rental truck, drove home, and crashed. I slept like a baby.

The Big Call

A week later, I got a phone call from Ed, the person who owned the décor and equipment Janelle had rented, wanting to know what had happened on Marco Island. Obviously someone had told him that things had not gone as planned. He proceeded to ask me a lot of questions about my life, my current job, and my past work experience. Then, to my absolute surprise, he offered me a job as display manager for his company. What the heck was a display manager? I had never set up a display in my life. The "manager" title was a bit exaggerated, as there was only one other person in the department, but I liked the idea of it. I accepted the job in September 1982, and that was the beginning of the next thirty years of setting up and producing live events.

Happily Ever After

I have often looked back on that fateful day on Marco Island, not fully understanding the chain of events that led me to getting that job. I always thought it was a simple case of being in the right place at the right time, and in a way it was. But the real reason Ed offered me the job that led to my lifelong career was my ability to recover from disaster. I had helped turn an event from a complete failure into a rousing success. Had I done what any sensible person would have done—wait for the storm to pass and then move the décor—Ed would never have known about the problem. I probably would never have been offered the display manager job at all. That night changed my life forever. Ed became my mentor for many years and taught me a lot about the business. I had to learn an awful lot more on my own—the hard way.

As I stated in the introduction of this book, in the live event business, you can plan until the cows come home, but at some point something is going to go sideways. And I'll say this over and over again: *The success or failure of the event will not be judged or measured by what went wrong, but by how fast you recover from the incident.*

The entire fire drill on Marco Island could have been avoided if someone had simply looked out the other side of the hotel or checked the weather forecast. Sometimes the most obvious things get overlooked. With today's weather technology available on your phone or tablet, you can eliminate this type of *surprise*. I emphasize the word *surprise*. Back then we had only the weatherman, and he was iffy at best. Whenever I am producing an outdoor event, I pay careful attention to weather forecasts that week, and especially the day before and morning of the event. Outdoor events are always risky endeavors. At some point, you will be forced to make a rain call to move the event inside, much to your attendees' or client's dismay.

It is a painful exercise to have spent the day setting up an outdoor event only to see dark clouds building on the horizon right before go time. The terrible thought hits you that you're going to have to take it all down and move inside. It is an even more painful exercise to see an event get completely wiped out because you didn't move it inside when you should have. You will, at some point, get caught in the middle of an event and have to watch it end with unhappy wet people. Once you live through one of these ordeals, you are much more confident when making tough decisions.

Now, when this situation begins to present itself, I check the radar, grab the client, and explain the obvious. I make it a joint decision. I use my standard line that is effective 99 percent of the time: "I have never had an event cancelled because it was moved inside." If the event starts and the weather fails to cooperate, there is usually little to no chance to salvage it. You'd better hope the place has a good lobby bar!

Size Matters

Back in the mid-1980s, four or five years into my event career, my firm was hired to produce an extremely extravagant, private event at the Sonesta Key Biscayne Hotel. It was a multiday event hosted by a man who was just shy of five feet tall. This gentleman wanted any new and edgy thing we could provide for the enjoyment of his 150 guests. The series of events culminated with a lavish dinner, including a large orchestra and entertainment headlined by Chubby Checker.

During the planning phase of this event, I was working on developing a lighted tabletop. The client had seen the prototype and wanted these tabletops for his final-night event. Back then, there was no LED or fancy high-tech way of doing it. I had built a seventy-two-inch round wood disc with a three-inch lip around it. I stapled white Christmas lights inside the wood disc and then set a seventy-two-inch round white Plexiglas top on the wood disc and lights. A sheer, floor-length linen was placed over the top of the lighted tabletop to complete the look of the new design. We did not have any type of wireless power sources, but had to actually run extension cords from each table to the power source. It was a very time-consuming process.

Fast-forward to the event's final night. I had completed the construction of the fifteen new, lighted tabletop designs and was eager to see them all set up in the room. The prototypes had been tested in the warehouse and were now ready to go. It was around four o'clock in the afternoon, and we had been working in the room all day getting everything ready. Chubby had sound-checked, and the client was doing a walk-through to check everything out prior to starting the event. He approached our new lighted tables with great excitement, as he was going to be the first person in the South Florida social scene to ever use this new event product. The gentlemen sat down, put his arms up on the table, and then proceeded to have a total meltdown. He started screaming that the tables were totally unacceptable and wanted to know if I was trying to embarrass him on purpose. I asked him what the problem was; he told me that the tabletop came up too high. Coming to the middle of his chest, it made him look even shorter than he already was.

Wow, I never saw that coming. Yes, it did raise the tabletop three and a half inches, but those of us who had tried it thought it was no issue. The only problem was that no one who had tried it was four feet, eleven inches tall.

His parting words to me were that the tables were completely unacceptable, and I had better fix the problem before the event started in two hours. Having faced only a few potential disasters in my early career, I was not that well armed with instant remedies. My staff and I looked like deer in the headlights, realizing that our new creation had just become a disaster. I went from hero to zero in one quick second.

We started fiddling with the chairs, trying to think of a way to raise his chair so he didn't look so low at the table. Unfortunately, we couldn't create a fix that didn't make him look like he was sitting in a booster chair. Then suddenly I had the bright idea to saw three and a half inches off the hotel table legs. That got ugly, since the hotel staff had already started to set the tables. I quickly had them remove all of the dinnerware; we flipped the tables and cut down all of the table legs exactly three and a half inches, using a hacksaw. It took nearly the entire two hours to complete this task, but by event time, they were the right height for this client.

Needless to say, the hotel's director of catering was absolutely furious. First, I dared to cut off the legs of his hotel tables; and second, I caused his staff to be delayed setting the tables for the evening event. In the end, the client was happy; the lowered tables almost sat on everyone's lap; and I bought new tables for the hotel. The crazy thing was that the hotel's catering director and I became friends, and I enjoyed a good working relationship at the hotel for years to come.

Anytime you are creating something new that has never been tried, I highly recommend having your client see it, try it, taste it, or touch it before you actually implement it. That goes for entertainment, too.

Why You Always Have a Plan B

The previous story is a perfect example of how you can never overplan. It also clearly illustrates the need for having a solid backup plan in place, just in case the unforeseen happens. In the following case, it did, and the end result was not pretty.

The location of the event was a large resort in the Bahamas, in November 2002. The event was the 2nd Annual Michael Jordan Celebrity Golf Tournament. The list of attendees was the who's who of sports, music, and television. They came to this event for a few days of golfing, beaches, parties, and pampering. The event was a fundraising golf outing, where corporate sponsors paid to play golf with the list of attending celebrities, as well as attend the fabulous parties.

The hotel had contracted me to take care of the event logistics for the opening welcome reception. The opening reception was a rather large outdoor affair, with food stations, bars, live entertainment, décor, and seating for 850 guests. The event was set on the beautiful lawn, right between the main pool and the ocean—quite a spectacular event location. As one of the in-house destination management and décor companies contracted at the hotel, we had produced several large events at this location previously. Events of this size usually require six to ten hours of setup to get all of the components in place prior to the start of the event. The scary thing about producing outdoor events in any tropical location is a small item called *weather*.

The first rule of planning any outdoor function is that you *must* always have a suitable backup location in case Mother Nature wants to mess with you that day. Typically, the planner or company that contracts the venue will also contract the backup space and ensure that it will fit the group size. In this case, the hotel was the planner and was also hosting the event. I never inquired into the location of the backup space, as they were the ones in control of it all.

The setup was coming to its conclusion. All elements were in place: lighting levels were set, food was out and on the food stations, bars were set and ready to go, and the staged and strolling entertainment was in place. The sun had just taken the rest of the day off, and the cool evening tropical breezes began to lightly blow. Shortly thereafter, throngs of guests streamed out onto the lawn from the main hotel, making their way to the beverage stations set up around the event space.

About fifteen to twenty minutes into the event, that nice little evening tropical breeze started to blow like the Wicked Witch from *The Wizard of Oz*. Dresses, skirts, and tablecloths lifted as the storm-chilled air unleashed a torrential rain of ridiculous intensity. Ole Mother Nature just dropped a bomb on this event; it looked like a scene from a disaster movie. People screamed and ran for cover. Unfortunately, the location of the event was a ten-minute walk (or a five-minute run) back to the cover of the main hotel. Along the way, a few small towel huts provided ten or fifteen people refuge from the storm.

Within a minute of the unleashing of this torrential downpour, everyone outside was absolutely soaked to the bone; I'm talking one massive wet T-shirt contest. I learned quickly that the "pretty people" do not like to look bad in front of other "pretty people," no matter what the circumstance. The attendees were suffering soaked clothes, ruined shoes, wrecked hair, and running makeup, never mind what the event looked like. Band gear was wrecked; all the food was toast; décor, linens, and flowers were soaked; and not one single salvageable item was left.

The hotel staff did the best they could to try and help the guests find cover, but there wasn't any cover without the long trek back to the air-conditioned hotel. The dripping-wet attendees started pouring back into the hotel, but they instantly froze upon entering the air-conditioned rooms. The hotel staff scrambled to find towels for everyone as they came back inside.

I ducked into a small 10x10 tent used for food service that was standing out on the lawn. As I popped into this small tent full of a lot of people, I found myself standing next to the CEO of the resort. By this time, it was probably fifteen minutes into the storm, and still raining so hard that the water was literally above our ankles. I could immediately see that the CEO wanted to be out of that tent and back at the hotel. He needed to see what the next step in salvaging this event would be. I offered him a ride on my golf cart; I warned him that it wouldn't be a completely dry ride, but it would be a fast one. I ran to my cart, jumped in, stopped by the towel hut for some dry towels, and picked up the CEO for a fast evac to the hotel. The hotel had strict policies regarding where I could drive that cart, but in this situation, I ignored them. I went right down the pool deck steps—bang, bang, bang—using the shortest route to get him there as quickly and dry as possible.

As I mentioned earlier, you should *always* have an indoor backup space ready in case of bad weather. The resort didn't have one, though, because it was full of corporate groups utilizing all of the available space. So instead, the evening didn't unfold so smoothly. The people who got drenched outside went back to their rooms, changed, and came back downstairs to the main lobby. All of the people who hadn't made it to the party yet had been hanging out in the lobby watching the theatrics. By this time, it was almost eight o'clock.

The big question then was where to feed 850 people. The restaurants were full, and there were no off-property options. The hotel did the best they could to try and accommodate those VIP guests, but it was a rather futile attempt. With that many people, it was nearly impossible to communicate with everyone; they had spread out all over the place. Needless to say, it was not a happy ending to the evening's event. The next day and the final night were great, and everyone looked back and laughed it off—kinda.

The hotel would never have let a paying customer produce an outside event without a backup location. Since this was their own non-revenue-generating, marketing-type event, they got caught in a bad way. They put themselves in a very uncomfortable situation, to say the least. I'm not really sure how Michael Jordan felt after experiencing that nightmare.

The lesson here is rather obvious: no matter what outdoor event you are planning, *always* have a backup plan and a place to go. Nine times out of ten you will be okay, but rest assured Mother Nature is waiting for the time that you have no backup.

Not Exactly Like Selling Ice to the Eskimos

In the early 2000s, while operating my destination management company and event production business in Nassau, I had the brilliant idea of setting up an ice centerpiece and sculpture operation. It made perfect sense to me. No one would ever expect to see ice centerpieces in a tropical destination, and hence, everyone would want to buy them. I had a friend who was in the ice business in Orlando, and we partnered up. We sent a complete ice manufacturing system to Nassau in order to begin operation.

After several weeks of shipping, setup, and training, we were finally ready to begin producing our custom ice centerpieces for special events (or so we thought). However, we still had several problems to overcome:

> **Problem 1** – Our first attempt to manufacture ice, which normally takes twelve to fourteen hours to freeze, was taking from twenty-four to forty-eight hours. After much diagnosis and troubleshooting, we determined that the ambient air

temperature was so high in our warehouse that it was taking two to three times longer to make the ice.

Solution – Buy fans and cooling for the warehouse to lower the temperature. This helped, but was not a complete fix.

► **Problem 2** – In order to be in the ice business, we needed large walk-in freezers to store the finished product. That required people (Bahamians) to go in and out of the freezer throughout the day and night. People of the islands *do not like the cold.*

Solution – Buy snowmobile suits and gloves for employees to wear in and out of the freezer. The problem was that these guys would be in a 28° freezer and then come out into a 120° warehouse about thirty times a day. Once again, not a great fix.

► **Problem 3** – In order to get the ice products to the event in the shape or form they were supposed to have, we needed a refrigerated truck. Each unit was packed in an insulated Styrofoam box that preserved the ice in transport. In the islands, there were no refrigerated trucks to rent or lease, and thus the trip had to be made with precise timing of freezer to table. The centerpieces had a life of about four to six hours in a 78° air-conditioned function space.

Solution – Attach a generator to our truck and put three window-unit air-conditioners in the box. Not a perfect fix, but it helped.

After dealing with a few weeks (months) of challenges, we finally gained our stride and started producing the ice product with some *moderate* consistency. I state moderate consistency. If any of you have ever spent much time in the Caribbean, or any country outside the United States, you may have incurred the frequent and usually temporary power outages.

Fast-forward a few months. We had a rather large order for eighty ice centerpieces to be used at a final-night awards dinner. That many ice sculptures would normally take a day or two for an operation stateside, but with our location challenges, they took about four days to make. The week before, we started making all of the ice sculptures for the event. We completed the order on time and made several extras, as well.

Our event was on a Monday evening; the crew went home on Friday with a freezer full of product, ready to be delivered. Unfortunately, sometime Friday night or early Saturday morning, there was a wreck near the warehouse that knocked down a power pole. The accident interrupted the power to the freezer for two days.

Monday morning, we arrived at the warehouse to see the floor covered in water. We painfully realized that all the ice in the freezer had melted and we had no centerpieces for this event. We could use our backup plan—floral centerpieces—but getting eighty large florals on the island the same day was no easy task. Floral inventory was flown in every two or three days, usually Tuesdays and Fridays. However, having no centerpieces for this high-profile awards event was not an option.

Solution – Mondays typically had very little local flower inventory after the weekend's events. Once we had exhausted every effort to find flowers on the island, we had no choice but to fly an order in from Florida. We are talking about flying in fresh flowers, having them clear customs, getting them to the local florist, and having them prepped, designed, and then delivered to the hotel in time for the event. We did it; the flowers were awesome, big vases of loose European-styled arrangements (which takes little design time). The cost was huge, but I saved a client. It was not what they had purchased, but after a brief explanation and a solid solution, they were fine with the change.

THE CALM BEFORE THE STORM (PHOTO BY DWJ)

ICE CENTERPIECES (PHOTO BY DWJ)

DARREN'S TIP

When you are staring in the face of adversity, never let money cloud your decision to implement the fix. You can always make the money back, but you may never get the client back.

Power: A Producer's Best Friend

Throughout this book, I know I have beat the proverbial horse (power) to death, but this story needs telling. It is not uncommon to find yourself producing an event at a venue or hotel where your power requirements exceed what the venue has available. Large events with extensive sound, lighting, video, and entertainment will eat up power very quickly. There may also be other users or venue needs for power in addition to your event.

I was involved in the production of a very large corporate event that required a significant audiovisual component. The AV required more power than the hotel had available, thus a large, quiet, diesel generator was contracted to provide supplemental power for the multiday event. The setup and on-site execution of the event progressed throughout the course of the week as it was supposed to; all systems were go, and there were no power issues whatsoever.

On the last day of the four-day event, during the morning general session, the video and the lighting went out in the middle of an executive presentation. The speaker continued to present due to the fact that the audio was still loud and clear. A quick-thinking backup spotlight operator hit the presenter with a spotlight. The executive only suffered about a ten-second period of darkness. The speaker concluded his on-stage presentation on time, and the morning session then went to a scheduled fifteen-minute break.

Needless to say, the entire production crew was scrambling to locate the power failure and quickly realized it was the generator that failed. It had actually run out of diesel fuel. The daily procedure, anytime you are operating on a generator, is to check the gas. Look every morning or at the end of the day to determine if a fill-up is needed. This procedure was in place; two different people had checked the fuel gauge, and each time they reported it was full. Unbeknownst to any of the crew, the gauge was broken and read full. Had a single person been checking the gauge, they might have noticed that the gauge was not moving. In this case, both guys thought the other had filled it.

As you can see, even when you have the best-laid plans, issues will find a way into your world. I cannot reiterate often enough that when producing a corporate event, close is never acceptable. It is not paranoia to have a backup plan or "what-if" procedure for every aspect of your event.

QUIET DIESEL GENERATOR (PHOTO BY DWJ)

Tip 1: Anytime you are using a generator as your power source for a multiday event, always schedule a fuel check and fill. Inspect not only the gauge, but do a visual inside the cap as well. Fuel gauges are notorious for giving false readings.

Tip 2: If not for the expertise of the technical director (TD) in charge of the production, the speaker's presentation could have been a train wreck. Two safety nets were put into place prior to the event. One was having a backup spotlight operator on house power, and the second safety net was not putting all of the AV needs on the same power source. Remember, audio is the first and most important component in technical production. A speaker or performer can perform in the dark, but it's "game over" if you lose the audio. In this case, the TD put the audio power on the house power, which would be the least likely to fail, and the lighting and video on the generator.

Remember...

- When an unexpected situation presents itself, embrace the opportunity to rescue the circumstance versus becoming part of the problem.

- You will have a much softer landing from an unforeseen incident if you have spent the proper time in the planning process. You cannot overestimate the value of pre-event planning.

- Always stay calm; if you look panicked, the client will panic, too.

- When producing outdoor events, you must always have a suitable backup location.

- Stay on top of weather forecasts.

- Do not let money cloud your decisions on a fix.

- When using generators, be diligent on fuel consumption and visual fuel inspections.

Chapter 8

Indoor Venue Tips

"Part of show business is magic. You don't know how it happens."

— Sammy Davis, Jr.

Indoor venues provide you with a safe, controlled environment, sheltered from Mother Nature. They also give you the ability to control the temperature inside the space. Indoor venues have a much higher rate of success than their counterpart outdoor venues. The ability to control climate and weather has yet to be mastered when producing outdoor events; therefore, the rate of success for indoor events is greatly increased.

In this chapter, I will focus on the four main indoor venues and a few funky spaces that I have worked in the most during my thirty-year career. Prior to selecting or working inside one of these venues, I highly recommended that you perform a thorough site inspection of your potential choice. It is extremely important to know the space's access, size, and limitations prior to beginning the planning process. The four most commonly used venues that host special events are hotels, convention and civic centers, music and entertainment venues, and country clubs.

These venues are the most frequently used sites in major metropolitan cities. While countless other indoor locations, from armories and auditoriums to barns and malls, make great event sites, I will focus on the ones most commonly used. Venues built in the last thirty years typically have thought through most of the event-related issues such as loading docks, load-in doors, ceiling heights, and electrical needs. I do say most places have addressed these issues, but not all. For the sake of being redundant, I am noting again the importance of double-checking the most critical issues. These include the room dimensions and measurements (not forgetting the ceiling heights) and power availability. While you are checking these concerns, you should also inquire about venue charges.

Pre-Function Area and Public Space

One of the very first areas you will most likely see while doing your site inspection is the *pre-function area* or foyer; this is generally shared public space. Ask the question "Is any part of it going to be used by another group during your event?" Is the wedding party next door going to be parading through your space to get to their space? Believe me, it happens all the time. Always ask about other events already booked in the venue. The person presenting the space may not always be forthcoming with that information.

DARREN'S TIP Always ask the venue you are considering for your event what other groups will be in-house, where they are, and exactly what they are doing. Knowing what is happening on the other side of that wall could have a bearing on the success of your event.

Walls, Ceilings, Floors, and Acoustics

Not all walls are created equal. There are air walls, hard walls, and glass walls, and every one of those will have a different impact on your event. Air walls are movable, semiacoustically insulated walls that travel on a track. They expand or retract, like an accordion. They allow the venue to easily close off or open up a space. Air walls are most common in big function spaces, and they are the most notorious for allowing noise between rooms.

Let's say your event is going to be in a hotel ballroom that divides into thirds using air walls. The hotel person will show you your event space and say, "This is where the wall closes," a nice, private space. Little do you know that on the other side of that air wall, there is going to be a wedding reception with a ten-piece band and a sound system flown from the ceiling. Your guests may not be thrilled with having to listen to the latest top-40 and hip-hop favorites while your CEO delivers the company's latest financial information. Always ask about sound integrity of the particular air walls, since there are many different types, with different-quality sound insulations.

Room acoustics are impacted by three primary things: the ceiling type, floor covering, and wall covering. Tall, exposed, or metal ceilings, concrete or tile floors, and bare block walls will all present issues to the event planner. They create acoustical challenges for an event that is going to provide any type of amplified entertainment or speaking. The problem with this type of venue is that the sound bounces off the floors and walls; it can create an echo effect that is less than desirable.

When providing amplified entertainment or speaking, the ideal venue is a room with some type of acoustical architectural ceiling, walls with carpet or panels, and a carpeted floor. These features absorb the sound and eliminate any type of echo or hollow sound. If budget is no problem, you can easily address any acoustical challenges by having carpet and décor treatments brought in. They will not only help with acoustics, but also enhance the look of the venue.

The next consideration is carpet. Some places have such crazy carpet designs and bold colors that you can't help wondering what they were thinking when they chose it. If you're planning an elegant event—perhaps an awards dinner with a lot of red décor—you're not going to want a space that has mauve and green jungle-print carpet from 1984.

Lighting

Another key consideration is lighting. Even though you'll conduct most of your site visits during the day, you still have to think about what it's going to look like at night. If you're doing a trade show, meeting, or seminar, fluorescent lighting is acceptable; you'll need as much light as you can get. But it is not ideal when you're trying to create a certain intimate mood or vibe. Heaven forbid you find out on the night of the event that the venue only has full-on, bright halogen or fluorescent lights that can't be dimmed. Find out about the different light settings, so they don't conflict with what you're trying to create. Try to visit at the same time your event is going to be held; this holds very true with spaces that have large glass windows. Remember to take daylight saving time into consideration, so you don't get a false reading.

Here is quick example of how big windows and setting suns can impact your event. A few years back, I produced an awards dinner at a Florida resort for a pharmaceutical company in late May. The location in the resort was selected by the client due to its large deck overlooking the Gulf of Mexico. This was an ideal spot for the cocktail reception that was to take place. Upon completion of the cocktail reception, everyone moved inside for the awards presentation and evening dinner. Once everyone was seated, the CEO began his slide presentation, with all the winners' info shown on the screen. About fifteen minutes into the awards presentation, the sun had dropped to a place where it shone like a giant searchlight—right on the screens in the room. The windows at ground level had large twelve-foot drapes, but the eight-foot transom windows above them did not. It took almost forty minutes for the sun to set enough to where the screens were in full visibility again.

Later that night, I asked the hotel if that had ever happened before. They said, "Only in the summer and if you set the stage the way it was set." Thanks for the heads-up. Luckily for me, I was not responsible for the production that evening. But my point is that big windows can create big problems if not carefully considered.

Load-In and Strike Schedule

One of the most important elements when it comes to indoor venues is the load-in and strike schedule. How and when will you get all the stuff into the building? Are there certain times or other restrictions for loading in and loading out? Let's say you want to have an event that starts at 6 p.m., but the site has another group in that space until 5 p.m. You might make that work, but you are walking the high wire with no safety net. You can't expect to gain access to a room at 5, load-in, set up, decorate, rehearse, get the band up and running, and sound check by 6. Why? Because when you cut your setup time that way, you don't have the opportunity to double-check everything. That confirmation is your insurance, your way of making sure it's all going to work. You don't want a breaker blowing just as the guests walk in the door because you didn't have time to verify the power supply.

DARREN'S TIP   Always ask what time you can get into the space for load-in. You may assume that the space is available first thing in the morning, but it might actually be occupied up to one hour prior to your event. Be sure to confirm and include the setup time as well as the event times when signing the venue contract.

Sometimes you won't have the luxury of seeing the location in advance, because you're working out of the country or out of state. In that case, you must arm yourself with all the right questions. Call the location, go through everything I have just addressed, and have them send you pictures of these areas. Pictures should include the foyer, overall room shots, carpet, ceiling, and chairs. Make sure that all of the elements are workable and that nothing stands in the way of achieving your event's goal.

Most people just walk through the door at an indoor event and never give a second thought to how all of the event components found their way inside that room. But as an event producer, one of the most important considerations I have is load-in. Many times we've been hired to produce an event, and for whatever reason, we did not have the luxury of inspecting the space in advance. We found out at the last minute that the size of the entry prevented us from bringing something important into the room.

A perfect example was a fiftieth anniversary celebration we handled for a car dealership at a client-selected location. We were supposed to pick up and bring in an enormous chocolate cake that the client had ordered. Unbeknownst to us, it was over six feet tall and six feet wide. We were assured that there were eight-foot-wide double doors that we could come through. When we got there, we discovered that the doorway was indeed eight feet wide—but it had a nonremovable center post, making each side less than four feet wide. We couldn't get the cake into the room in one piece no matter what we tried. We ended up sawing the cake in half; the cake maker had to come down and rebuild it inside the room. Load-in doorways are often overlooked when producing an event in an atypical indoor space. Always check out those load-in doors.

Always check out the ceiling, too—not only the height, but also how it is constructed and what it's made of. If you're going to suspend or hang décor, lighting, or sound equipment, the ceiling must have the structural integrity to support that kind of weight. It must also have places from which you can hang these elements. The places in a ceiling that are intended to support this equipment are called "hang points." You can't hang anything weighty from acoustical drop ceilings, as they cannot support any weight. Some locations have the old tin-stamped ceilings that cause everything you say to echo, so keep that in mind, too. When hanging equipment or items that are large or heavy, you will probably need a rigging company.

Venue Charges

Venue charges are the fees levied by hotels, country clubs, convention centers, auditoriums, and music locations to cover the cost of hosting your event. These charges are in addition to the room rental, and they can be pretty hefty. These charges vary greatly between venues, and many do not have any additional charges. So it pays to ask lots of questions before you sign on the dotted line and book a venue.

Supervisory Charges

More and more locations are now charging for a supervisor to sit in the room and watch you load-in, set up, and load-out. The venue is not doing that just to generate extra revenue, although it may seem that way. They are doing it to ensure that you don't cause any damage to the place when you're loading in, setting up, or taking down. Running carts into the doorjambs, hammering or screwing things into the walls, breaking light fixtures, ripping and staining carpets—well, shit happens, and it costs the venue money to make repairs. So it's understandable that they want someone there to keep an eye on those things.

The problem is that supervisor charges can be substantial. Let's say the supervisor charge is $80 per hour. If you're doing a two- or three-day event with multiple turns that requires a supervisor to be there for forty hours, before you know it, you've got a $3,200 bill on your hands. If you don't see them coming, these charges can blow your budget. I recently produced a four-day event in a resort hotel, and they not only charged for a supervisor in the ballroom, but also for an elevator operator and a loading-dock supervisor. Go figure!

Rigging Companies

Nowadays, if you plan on suspending (flying) any sound equipment, lighting, trusses, signs, or banners, venues often require you to hire a rigging company to facilitate those services. These outfits are contracted by the site to ensure that anything suspended from the ceiling is hung in a safe manner and affixed to something that can structurally support it. This is for safety and insurance purposes. The costs associated with rigging can be quite surprising, especially if you're hanging multiple trusses. I recommend that you get a handle on that fee right up front, because it can blow your budget in a hurry.

The only way around having to hire a location's rigging company is to ground support everything. Instead of flying (that's industry-speak for hanging) lighting from the ceiling, you put it on towers. Instead of suspending your signs or banners, you put them on easels. Aesthetically it's not the best option, but sometimes the budget mandates that you find other ways of displaying things versus hanging them from the ceiling.

Rigging companies are costly, but as I have mentioned before, so is power.

Power

Power at a venue can be a substantial cost that needs careful consideration in the budget planning process. This is probably the single biggest surprise that event producers and clients get from venues and hotels *after the fact*. Electric costs are not typically spelled out on the front end, or if they are, they're commonly miscalculated or misunderstood. For instance, they'll tell you that the charges for electric are $150 for a 20-amp or 2,000-watt circuit, plus labor. That may not sound like much until you realize that your vendors need thirty 20-amp circuits to get their jobs done. This may include the sound and lighting for the band, the photo stations, and all the many different elements that go into supporting the event. Suddenly you realize they've ordered thirty circuits at $150 each, and you've got a $4,500 electric bill on your hands. Believe me, that really has a way of making planners and producers hot. Always be aware that charges for electricity can be large, and plan accordingly.

Other venue-related charges that you should expect concern parking fees—for the guests as well as the production company.

Parking

Here's another one for the lesson file related to venue charges. Recently we produced an event at a hotel. It was a large event, where we had over sixty staff members in attendance working various gambling, gaming, and audience-participation activities. Self-parking at the hotel was $15. That doesn't sound like much until you consider that it was *$15 times sixty people*. Suddenly I had a parking bill—just to park my staff for five hours—of $900. That's something you would hopefully budget for on the front end, but it can bite you in the butt if you're not expecting it.

Public parking at most sites is generally readily accessible and has to meet certain requirements based on local code. This does not mean it is free, and you should always check on the cost of car parking at the location you are considering. Many of today's venues were not originally designed for hosting events, and sometimes parking is a real problem. If you are hosting a public event, be especially vigilant about parking arrangements. Your guests are driving in, and parking fees can be a huge deterrent if you have not arranged free parking with the site in advance. I have seen public events result in dismal attendance due to expensive parking fees that were not considered on the front end. This is especially prevalent in downtown areas. If folks pull in and find out that the location charges $25 to $50 a day to park a car, they may just pull right back out again. People have to park; that's a necessary evil when producing events with public attendance. Sometimes you can negotiate parking fees and get a discount. Sometimes you can even get them waived for event attendees—but not if you don't think of it when you're still in the planning stages.

If parking is not easily accessible, it is my recommendation to hire a valet company. Make sure you get copied as an additional insured on their insurance, and require more staff than they recommend. Coming into the event is not as much of a problem as leaving. Cars trickle in over a thirty-minute window at the beginning of the event start time, but everyone generally leaves at the same time. You *do not* want your guests waiting more than ten minutes for their car. Having people waiting too long for their cars is a really easy way to screw up a great event, especially if there is inclement weather.

Truck Parking

When you are producing an event in a resort environment, there is usually plenty of space (a marshaling yard) to accommodate truck parking. But that changes if you're at a convention center, auditorium, music venue, country club, or hotel in an urban environment. You are most likely going to be required to park at an off-site location because of space constraints, especially if you have a few big trucks or tractor-trailers. This can become a real headache—and a rather large expense—if you haven't settled it in advance. You may have six tractor-trailers that have to be parked for several days. The site may tell you that you have to go thirty miles down the road to park, which could cost $150 a day for parking each truck. If you are doing a four-day event and have six trucks—*bam!* You've just spent $3,600 for truck parking. So before you contract with that location, find out where you're going to park trucks and how much it's going to cost.

Before you park the trucks, however, you have to unload them at the site, using the location's loading docks.

Loading Docks

Loading docks are typically at the back of a venue, where trucks pull in and unload goods—supplies, food, beverages, and equipment for the event. No location wants to see event staff standing around out front or trucks unloading gear in sight of the public. You must always check and find out details about the loading dock situation.

The first thing you want to learn is how many loading docks there are. You may not think that's a relevant question, but if the venue gets all of its food deliveries from 9 a.m. to 2 p.m. every day and you have trucks scheduled to roll in at 10 a.m. to start setting up, there could be a logjam. You must coordinate your arrival and departure with the site because guess what: Their trucks will have priority over yours. Their food will be allowed to come in, and your trucks will have to sit and wait until they leave. So it's critical to know not only how many loading docks there are, but also the scheduling or the timing of the load-in.

Many event sites—most notably those above the ground floor of a hotel or office building—require you to load into freight elevators. Freight elevators create a few additional issues that you have to deal with. It takes about twice as long to load in and set up an event when you have to load into an elevator. Getting into the building, onto the elevator, going up, passing through hallways and kitchens, and blah, blah, blah—it just takes longer than normal. You'll likely incur more labor costs from your suppliers as well.

And of course, as we've already discussed, the most critical issue with freight elevators is the problem of gear and equipment not fitting inside. A lot of times you'll be forced to use a venue's service elevator, which is not really a freight elevator at all. It holds two or three room-service food carts. You won't be getting in there with a twelve-foot ladder or any big pieces of gear or lighting. So let me reiterate from earlier pages: If at all possible, it is *critical* that you find out the dimensions of service elevators before you book a venue.

(PHOTO BY DWJ)

Remember...

- Remember the huge chocolate cake–and always measure doors and service elevators.

- Ask about sound insulation and find out about events booked on the other side of the wall.

- Can you live with the color and design of the carpeting?

- Is the lighting dimmable?

- Where, when, and how will you get everything loaded in and out of the building?

- What are the venue charges?

- Where is truck parking, and how much will it cost per truck, per day?

- Where is guest parking and how much is it?

- Get electrical needs from all vendors early to get the electrical charge estimate.

- Get the rigging estimate prior to the event, while in the planning phase.

CHAPTER 9

The Great Outdoors

"All animals except man know that the ultimate point of life is to enjoy it."

— Samuel Butler

As a true Florida native (well, more than forty years of my life), I love the outdoors and sunshine. Florida winters are absolutely awesome and provide some of the best winter weather in the country. That is exactly why so many corporate groups choose to host their events in Florida from October through May. Needless to say, most residents north of the Mason-Dixon Line are pretty fed up with their weather come January. They will grab the chance to get as much of the Florida sunshine and nighttime balmy breezes as they can get. Hence the insatiable desire to hold group events outside, allowing their attendees the opportunity of enjoying this fabulous weather.

Whether at a beach, a desert, a mountaintop, a baseball stadium, or viewing a body of water, outdoor venues provide spectacular scenic backdrops for truly memorable events. I have produced about every imaginable type of event outside, from welcome receptions to award ceremonies, concerts to full-blown theme parties. The possibilities are limitless–but so are the risks.

Along with these amazing scenic backdrops comes the inherit risk of Mother Nature. The many evil little tricks in her bag can greatly affect the outcome of your event. Her inventory consists of rain, wind, snow, rising tides, insects, wild animals, and even hurricanes. In this chapter, I will share some of my lessons, experiences, and favorite outdoor venues.

Weather

One of the most important considerations when planning an outdoor event is the weather. What are the seasonal trends at this location? What time of day is the event going to be held? Is it going to be hot, cold, or something in between? What about rain? What about wind? What about bugs?

When it comes to the weather and outdoor events, you have to be on top of your game to ensure that there are no surprises—or at least, as few surprises as possible. You don't have to be a fortune-teller to be successful in this business, but you do have to be on your toes and know where to look for the most reliable information. You can find everything you need to know about long-range weather trends on *The Old Farmer's Almanac* website at www.almanac.com. It's an easy, inexpensive way to get information regarding typical weather trends.

A week before the event, set aside the almanac and start monitoring the weather forecast. You want to pay special attention to fronts moving across the states. I like Weather Underground (www.wunderground.com) for those days leading up to the event, but on the day before and morning of the Big Show, I switch to live Doppler radar.

DARREN'S TIP   Whenever I arrive in a city to host an event, I find a local TV affiliate and download its animated radar app to my smartphone. That way I'm always in the loop about the weather.

Pool Decks and Lawns

Some of the nicest events we've done have been on pool decks and lawns at hotels and other locations. But these venues present some unique issues that you have to keep in mind if you want to be successful and avoid headaches.

The first and foremost issue to address with the person in charge of the site is how early you can set up. This is a big deal. I estimate that 80 percent of hotels will refuse to close their pool deck and allow you to start setting up before 3 p.m. They have guests sunbathing in lounge chairs, and they don't want to have to displace them. And even if they do agree to close the pool deck before 3, that doesn't mean all the sunbathers and swimmers will leave. So you have to be careful when picking an outdoor pool deck venue, and get the site's assurance that they will close the pool deck early enough to give you ample time to load in and set up. This will usually be determined by how much of the hotel you occupy, and also whether or not your guests are at the pool.

The next issue is a biggie for events held on a lawn, whether it's at a hotel, on a golf course, at a country club, or on a stadium field. That issue is sprinklers. Sprinklers are one surefire way to screw up a good event. They really put a *damper* on things (sorry, I couldn't resist).

Picture this: On the day of the event, you're thinking you have all the bases covered. You've talked with the venue people, the catering contact, the engineering department, and the groundskeeper to make sure the sprinklers were shut off. And then they come on in the middle of your event anyway. I can tell you—it happens. It definitely happens.

I've seen entire wedding parties—the bride, the groom, the cute little flower girls, the elderly grandparents, and even the clergyman—soaked to the bone in seconds. I've seen the food get entirely wiped out and the décor ruined. I've seen all kinds of crazy things happen at equestrian centers, baseball stadiums, parks, golf courses, and any place that has a grass lawn. So if you want to do a grass lawn event, you must check, double-check, and *triple-check* that those sprinklers are shut off. Because here's the deal: Someone will promise you they shut them off, or they'll swear to you that somebody else shut them off, and then suddenly you hear a bunch of shrieking and screaming. You turn around to see the undeniable proof that *no one shut the damn things off after all.*

Yet another lawn issue is damage to the grass. I've seen some enormous bills incurred at an outdoor event that caused substantial lawn damage. This typically results from crushing the grass under a stage or dance floor, from driving trucks on the grass, and from dragging stuff across it. You have to ask in advance about what will happen if the lawn gets damaged. Some places accept that the grass is going to take a beating and they simply resod and move on. Other places absolutely freak out, as if you just drowned a litter of puppies.

DARREN'S TIP

Whether or not you will be subject to lawn damage charges or not, always do your best to avoid wrecking the lawn. One way to mitigate damage is to lay down plywood. You can then roll carts and drive vehicles on top of that, not directly on the grass.

Another important consideration when it comes to pool decks and lawns is cabling—the cords that go from your power source to the electrical equipment that need power in order to run. This can include anything from the heat lamps and coffee stations on the buffets to the lighting for the decorations. It may be the audio and lighting for the band, or any other element that requires electricity. Running cable is not as straightforward as it sounds. Sometimes the power source is a long way from the actual equipment. You have to make sure that your cabling never goes in front of any doorways or other high-traffic areas where people could trip on them. You can't avoid cables entirely, but you can take the time to plan in advance where you'll put them, so they're less likely to cause a mishap. Make sure you include cable placement in the CAD that you draw up for the event.

The next item in this category is noise curfews. Just about every venue, municipality, and city has some type of restriction on how late you can have music playing at outdoor events. It's only an issue if you want to go later than the ordinance allows. So before booking any outdoor venue, always ask, "What are the noise curfews for this space?"

Another potential sticking point (literally!) is glass. Most venues prohibit the use of glass on or around pool decks for obvious reasons. If you're planning an upscale dinner or a wine tasting and your client doesn't want to drink or eat from plastic, then you'll need to reconsider the pool deck as a venue. Lawns aren't usually as restrictive when it comes to glassware. But some still prohibit it in any space where people will be barefoot later, whether it's a playground or a lawn that people cross to get to a beach or a pool. If using glass is important to you or your client, then you need to know about those restrictions before the event. Nowadays, there are decent alternatives in the form of nice plastic stemware, drinkware, and plates, which look classier than the usual flimsy plastic. Still, some folks adamantly refuse to use plastic at their event. If your client is one of those and glass is forbidden at a particular venue, you may have to choose another locale for their event.

Parks

Parks can be very much a hit-or-miss proposition when it comes to producing live events. Every city, state, and federal park has different guidelines and rules that must be adhered to in order to produce an event. I have produced an event at a city park and then gone back to produce another corporate event a few months later, only to find that a completely different set of rules was in place. You have to ask for the rules in advance every time, even if it's the tenth time you've produced an event there.

Anytime you're considering booking a public park for an event, know that there are going to be a lot more restrictions than there would be in a privately owned space. For example, we have done events on public beaches where you could have no lighting after nine o'clock at night because of sea turtle nesting. We've had issues with noise curfews due to bald eagle nesting. Many parks have restrictions on alcohol consumption, but others don't. There are all kinds of not-so-nice surprises awaiting you on the day of the event if you don't ask the right questions during the prebooking stage.

DARREN'S TIP   Get a list of rules from the park people. Meet with them and ask if there are any unusual circumstances or restrictions that happen at different times of the year, because what may be acceptable today may be prohibited in another season.

Stadiums

I love producing events at outdoor stadiums. Professional football stadiums, spring training baseball parks, and racetracks are great because they're built to accommodate crowds. They have the parking. They have the security. They have the restrooms. They have the ability to do fireworks. They have city approval to host big, loud events because that's what they were built for. And they are usually privately owned, so you can do pretty much whatever you want—within reason, of course. There is a nice price tag associated with all those perks, but to me it's worth it.

Here again, the number one concern a stadium has when it comes to hosting events is the lawn care. After all, that surface is their most valuable asset—whether the stadium is home to a football, soccer, or baseball team. So you have to be very sensitive to that when loading gear in and out of there. Take preventive measures like rolling equipment in and out on plywood or decking. Also, note that there are sprinkler heads on a playing field, and the stadium folks get really ticked off when you bust those. Finally, remember to check once, twice, twenty times to make sure those sprinklers have been disabled for the duration of your event.

Load-ins at stadiums are typically easy. Usually there is a big gate in the outfield that allows you to gain easy access. But we have been to stadiums where they would not let us onto the grass from the outfield. The only way we were allowed in was through the locker rooms. We had to navigate a maze of corridors, working our way to the dugout and onto the infield. There were no ramps on which to wheel equipment, and we literally had to carry our stuff up and down the stairs. So be aware of how you're going to get gear in and out of the stadium, especially if it's in a downtown setting. Those locations tend to be tight.

Power can be tricky in stadiums. You'll have no problems if you're up in the skyboxes or suites. You *will* have a problem if you need any kind of big power for outdoor staging or concerts. The exact place you need juice the most—on the field—is typically where there isn't any. You'll likely have to hire an outside electrical company to provide generators.

One of the great benefits of holding events at a stadium is being able to use the scoreboards. Most have one or more LED "Jumbotrons" that you can customize with the name of the company, its top performers or loyal customers, or any other brand message. You can show a welcome message, video of commercials, and any other marketing or media content you might have. It costs little or nothing to get those boards programmed. All you have to do is get the content on a jump drive or CD from your client's marketing department and give it to the stadium folks. Their scoreboard or media operators will load it up. Presto! Your client's name is in lights!

A great event at a stadium is to hire a Legends baseball team and have your

attendees play them for a three- or four-inning game. Arrange for the concession vendors to give away popcorn, sodas, pretzels, and such during the game. Afterward, all of
the Legends players will stay, eat dinner, tell stories, and sign autographs for your guests.
Needless to say, a killer fireworks show with a logo burn would be a terrific grand finale
for an event like this. This type of thing really leaves an awesome, lasting impression on
those who were lucky enough to be in attendance.

DARREN'S TIP   Clients love tours of locker rooms—especially if you've
gone in ahead of time, put their names on the lockers, and
stuffed goodie bags inside. You can have personalized
jerseys made for them, or put their branding on the outfield
wall. You could even have autographed bats or footballs
for them...Can you tell I dig working in stadiums?

Theme Parks

Theme parks are an awesome location for corporate events and can provide unmatched wow factors. With these unmatched wow factors also come a variety of logistical challenges. Theme parks are very strict when it comes to setup hours due to the fact
that their park guests are all over the place. You'll have to live with some very short
setup times. That impacts how much stuff you can actually set up, and the park may
have restrictions on who or what you can bring in as well.

Power can be another challenge, because there usually isn't much other than what
is needed for normal park operations. You'll need to bring electricity into those areas
by running cabling, and here again arise the safety issues we covered before. You have
to be very aware of where those cables are running and make sure they're not in any
hot-traffic areas.

When it comes to load-in, how are you going to get to the middle of the theme
park from the back gates? It can sometimes be daunting. You'll go through tunnels,
down back alleyways, and around parts of the park that you didn't even know existed.
It's rarely a simple, straight shot, I can tell you that. Here again, it always pays to do a
proper site visit prior to executing your event.

And then there are the rules. There are lots and lots and lots of rules, and it's your
job to find out what they are. It's also your job to make sure everyone else knows what
they are, too. You do not want to make a promise to your client about what can be done
at a theme park and find out the day of the event you are not allowed to do it. Always
reconfirm with your theme park representative prior to making a promise to your client
you can't fulfill.

Those are some of the challenges to producing an event in a theme park. However, there is one major benefit, and it's a doozey: you get to take advantage of all of the park's existing client branding opportunities, entertainment, audio, lighting, rides, food, and beverages. The trick is to create an event at the theme park that the typical guest cannot get on his or her own. Most theme parks have now developed an extensive menu of special event items, such as entertainers, firework shows, custom branding, characters, and parades for those unique guest experiences. It's a very special and memorable place to do an event—if you have a good budget and a bit of patience.

Beaches and Islands

Because I have worked in Florida and the Caribbean for so long, I have produced a ton of events on beaches and islands. Over the years, nature has thrown quite a few curveballs my way during these events. But I've learned a few tricks of the trade that will help make your beach or island event a spectacular success.

Have you ever heard the old saying "A rising tide lifts all boats"? Well, I'm here to tell you that a rising tide will also lift your event's décor, your tables, your food, your guests' shoes and handbags, and everything else within its reach–and trust me, you don't want that. So anytime you're doing an event on a beach or island, you must be aware of the tidal range for that time of year. You may visit a beach in December and see a high tide that's thirty feet away from where you're planning to do your event in the springtime. If you think that everything will be high and dry on your event day, you couldn't be more wrong. If there is a full moon or an exceptionally high tide, you could find that same exact space completely underwater in March.

DARREN'S TIP You can find projected U.S. tide heights, sunrise, and moonrise information for up to a year in advance at www.saltwatertides.com.

I once produced a beach event when the tide came in and went halfway up onto the tables where the guests were sitting. It didn't come in fast, like a tsunami. It happened gradually over a period of about an hour, during which time it just kept coming and coming and coming. There was a full moon that night, with a wind pushing the tide even farther onshore. I already knew there was going to be a high tide, but I didn't think of the full moon or onshore winds. Luckily the event wasn't a total washout because the guests were good-natured about it. They picked up the tables and chairs, and we moved them farther up the beach. We were able to turn a negative into a positive—other than the fact that the bottom half of the women's pants and dresses were wet and a few of their shoes were ruined.

The next thing to consider when it comes to beaches and islands is flying bugs. If you've ever done evening events in the Caribbean or in Florida, you already know that insects like no-see-ums, mosquitoes, and flies can be a nuisance at certain times of the year. I have learned this lesson many times over. When Mother Nature wants your attention, she can devise some pretty stunning ways to get it.

Such as the time she sent so many bugs to my events that the guests and I felt like we were in a horror movie. It happened during an outdoor event on Great Exuma Island, in the Bahamas. We were barbecuing lobster and steak on a huge deck, right on the ocean; everything was going great. We had just pulled the food off the grill and were preparing to serve when suddenly, out of nowhere, came an infestation of flies the likes of which I have never seen before or since. It was a massive swarm of what appeared to be millions of flies—and they were the attacking kind. I'm talking about a fly swarm of biblical proportions. The guests were literally screaming because there were so many flies in their hair, on the food, all over their bodies—they were everywhere. Everyone grabbed their plates and ran inside the house; thankfully, we had a place to go. Keep in mind that this was not some beach picnic with everybody in T-shirts and flip-flops. This was an ultraexclusive event, and it turned into a total fiasco.

Even in hindsight, I don't know what we could have done differently. Maybe we could have lit 10,000 citronella torches or candles versus the forty we had, or used more propane as a repellant to minimize the negative impact of bugs. Who knows? Those were some pretty determined flies. The truth is, you can put out as many candles and insect repellents as you want, but if any of your guests are allergic to those particular bugs or prone to getting bitten, it can put a damper on your event. And therein lies the lesson: You want to avoid mingling with those insects in the first place. Just because you don't see insects during your site visit doesn't mean they won't be there later.

LOCATION OF INVASION OF FLIES (PHOTO BY DWJ)   LOCATION OF INVASION OF FLIES (PHOTO BY DWJ)

DARREN'S TIP Always secure everything you use on a beach or island as if the wind is blowing hard. That way you won't have too many surprises when it does.

The next big issue on beaches and islands is wind. That nice, gentle, tropical breeze that's barely rustling the palm fronds on the morning of your event can turn into a thirty-knot gale after the sun goes down. Here again, there are seasonal trends that will help you know what to expect, so look at the almanac and ask around. Is it windy that time of year? What about prevailing winds on your chosen side of the island?

During the setup of these events, you always want to secure every item as if it were already blowing twenty knots. So often, I see events get set when there is no breeze, and then the crew leaves before the event starts. Then the wind picks up as the sun goes down. Next thing you know, the décor is toppling, the linens and centerpieces are blowing away, and the possibility of a dangerous situation is imminent.

This brings us to sand. Some people love sand between their toes; others hate it. But one thing is unanimous—we all hate sand blowing in our faces and in our food. This is just another reason to be diligent about knowing the wind trends.

Also, realize that when you set tables and other things on the sand, they have a tendency to lean. Food and drinks will fall off cockeyed tables, so keep that in mind. The most important issue when planning a beach or island event on sand is to be considerate of your guests. How will they be dressed? Are they going to be casual and barefoot, or more formal with shoes on? Sand can be a real pain for people who aren't dressed appropriately for it.

And finally, we're back to our old friend (or nemesis!): power. Actually, power is an issue just about every place you go, but especially on the beach because there is none. So, know that you're going to bring in generators and there is going to be cabling to deal with. The good thing about cabling on the beach is that you can dig a trench and put it all under the sand. Problem solved!

Parking Lots

Parking lots may sound like an odd place to do corporate events, but we have actually done many and it has worked out great. Think about it: An event in a parking lot is along the same lines as a tailgate party, and everybody loves those. It could be a parking lot at a stadium, racetrack, mall, store, or hotel. Almost any parking surface can serve as a great location for an event. Usually we erect some type of large tent structure to house the event. Remember that you're probably going to bring in portable restroom trailers and have the power issue to deal with, but as long as you've got the potties, generators, and cabling issues covered, it's "all systems go."

However, you really have to be strategic and creative in setting up your logistical support unless you have a large tent. In a wide-open space like a parking lot, without a tent you have no place to hide your production, storage, food, and beverage equipment. Be thinking about that from the start.

The Desert

There are few places on earth more beautiful than the Southwest's desert, making it a perfect setting for an outdoor event. It's unique, and whenever we've done desert events, our clients and their attendees have really loved them. There are a lot of challenges associated with this locale; just like the beach and islands, you have to plan accordingly.

One of the biggest challenges in desert events, especially in the winter, is temperature fluctuation. You may have a seventy-five or eighty-degree day, but after nightfall the temperature will plummet to a bone-chilling thirty degrees. It's just crazy. Don't count on what you see and feel during your site inspection. Do the research and find out how much the temperature drops out there at night.

Another concern with desert events is wildlife, and I happen to have a story that highlights this topic perfectly. Once upon a time, we produced a three-part event out in the desert for a very important client. The event was going to kick off with a cocktail reception in a barn. We created a stunning Remington art gallery; the guests could wander through and enjoy the art while they indulged in tasty horsd'oeuvres and libations. Following the cocktail reception, dinner would be served under the desert sky around large fire pits, with the chefs cooking right beside the tables. After dessert, there would be a short walk over a ridge, where the guests would sit and enjoy a Kenny Loggins concert.

It was late afternoon on the day of the event, and my clients had just pulled up to do a walk-through with me before their guests arrived. As I was heading out to meet them, my staff called me into the barn and told me that there was a problem. Coiled up in the corner of the barn were two gigantic, fat rattlesnakes. There had been a cold spell over the previous few days that had forced many animals to seek warmth. These two enormous rattlesnakes had chosen the barn that was about to be the scene of my upcoming, exclusive cocktail party.

"You've got to kill these snakes right now," I said to my guys, whose eyes were as big as dinner plates. "The clients are on their way, and if they see this, they'll absolutely freak out."

Two of my staff members, who were Native American, shook their heads. One of them said, "No, we can't do it. In our culture, it is bad luck to kill rattlesnakes."

"Listen," I replied, "the bad luck will be that if you don't kill those snakes right now, we won't get paid this week. That's bad luck!"

I turned to go outside, where I met the clients and stood between them and the barn, stalling for time while my guys disposed of the snakes. I made up silly stuff about everything under the sun—the past, present, and future weather...desert sunsets...cactus flowers...until I saw my people coming out of the barn with a shovel and a black garbage bag full of dead rattlesnakes. The rest of the event went off without a hitch.

The moral of the story is this: Think about the wildlife when doing outdoor events. After all, you're partying in their backyard. Plan accordingly, and always keep your eyes peeled for uninvited guests.

COCKTAIL RECEPTION. HOME OF THE BIG RATTLESNAKES (PHOTO BY DWJ)

CONCERT AFTER DINNER (PHOTO BY DWJ)

DINNER AROUND FIRE PIT (PHOTO BY DWJ)

Remember...

- Use the Internet and local radar apps to stay on top of the weather.

- Memorize this sentence: "I have never had an event cancelled because it was moved inside."

- Check, double-check, and triple-check sprinklers.

- Discuss the potential for lawn damage so you and the venue know what to expect.

- Make sure cabling doesn't create a tripping hazard.

- Ask about noise curfews.

- Is glass allowed?

- Are there any special restrictions, such as wildlife protection measures?

- Use the scoreboard or Jumbotron to reinforce your client's message or brand.

- Take tidal range into consideration, as full moons create the highest (and lowest) tides, and onshore winds, especially in shallow water, can create what is known as a "blow-in" tide.

- Conversely, strong offshore winds can create blowout tides, leaving stinky sand and scurrying crabs for the party!

- Ask locals and the venue about potential insect or wildlife problems.

- Remember temperature fluctuations and wildlife in the desert.

CHAPTER 10

Funky Spaces

"I've been things and seen places."

– Mae West

Funky spaces are unique and nontraditional spaces that can be used or converted for some type of event. Their original design or purpose may be one thing, but to repurpose them as event space can be quite spectacular. Funky spaces are some of my favorite places to produce events. A funky space may be a historical venue, such as a castle or fort, a museum or cultural center, or even floating vessels, such as cruise ships, yachts, and barges. If you want or need to create a unique event, start with a unique or funky space. These venues will generally increase attendance and provide a memorable "wow" factor for the guests.

Museums

Whether they're designed to showcase art, history, science, aviation, or cars, museums offer a distinctive environment in which to host corporate events. Depending on the client and the guest list, it's relatively easy to find a museum that fits the event's goal in almost any locale. Just check the city's museum guide for a list of possibilities. I especially enjoy producing events in private museums because they have fewer restrictions. You also have a lot more flexibility with operating times and setup times than you do with those museums that are city-owned or public.

One of the coolest and most unique events I ever produced was a VIP luncheon in Yorba Linda, California, at the Richard Nixon Presidential Library and Museum. The location is Nixon's birthplace and where he and his wife, Patricia, are buried. We transported all of the guests to the venue in a motorcade of SUVs, complete with actors posing as uniformed Secret Service agents. When the guests—who were my client's top customers—arrived at the museum, they were greeted with a red carpet and a color guard carrying flags and rifles. They were led inside the museum, where they had lunch in an exact replica of the East Room of the White House—very presidential, histori-

cal, and grand. The guests were able to tour the grounds after the luncheon and see Nixon's house, as well as the Marine One helicopter and limousines that the former president rode in. It was an impactful venue; in fact, the site is what really drove the whole thing. The attendees loved it.

The chances are good that attending an event in a place like that will be a new experience for most of your guests, and

DARREN AT THE RICHARD NIXON MUSEUM EVENT (PHOTO BY KMJ)

uniqueness is always a plus. There are a few potential drawbacks to these locations, however. Museums and aquariums are not perfect for events requiring one big space because they tend to be chopped up into smaller rooms. Guests will be in different areas, but that may be fine with the event goal. As long as there's good continuity and flow between the rooms, you can make it work. Try to avoid rooms and spaces that feel disjointed from the main event.

One budget challenge with museums is that you will probably have to rent every single piece of equipment that you need to host the event. An additional challenge you may have to deal with is finding a location for catering. Museums rarely have back-of-the-house or kitchen facilities, so you'll have to set up a tent in the parking lot or another adjacent space for the food prep. These venues also expect perfection when it comes to post-event cleanup, so plan accordingly.

Airplane Hangars and Warehouses

Two of my all-time favorite venues are airplane hangars and warehouses. I love a space that's open and cavernous, with big, high ceilings. It really gives you a blank palette with which you can create just about anything. When I think of hangars and warehouses, I think impact—major impact. We've done some really cool events in both of these environments.

For example, we once rented an old space across from the New Orleans Convention Center that had been a sugar mill and warehouse in its heyday. This place was a bit dilapidated on the outside, but it was full of Big Easy charm. It was constructed from gorgeous red brick, with rustic wrought-iron gates and a high brick wall running around it. All in all, it was an awesome location.

But what made it stunning was what we did to the inside. We transformed that shabby old warehouse into a high-tech rave party for about 500 guests. On the outside it was extremely underwhelming and low-key, but inside we had theatrical lighting, a monster sound system, several different bands, all kinds of unique décor, and stylish lounge-type seating. Nobody would ever have guessed that a building like that could be transformed in such a way. It was a great event, and it was a winner because we took a nontraditional venue and converted it into something that made everyone go *"Wow!"* when they walked in the door.

Here's another example to get you thinking about possibilities. We took an airplane hangar and created a big, 1940s-themed USO event inside of it. It was 100 percent All-American Yankee Doodle Dandy patriotic in every way. We had tons of red, white, and blue banners and balloons everywhere. We brought in a cappella singers, a big swing band, and Andrews sisters' look-alikes. There were World War II airplanes, trucks, and Jeeps, with authentic weaponry mounted on board. The guests thoroughly enjoyed every minute of it. They'd never seen anything like it. And that's what you're shooting for every time—a new experience for your guests.

DARREN'S TIP — Look for a unique, counterintuitive venue that lends itself to generating that "wow" impact when guests first walk in the door. Think total immersion, total transformation. Think outside the norm. Think funky spaces.

NEW ORLEANS WAREHOUSE EVENT (PHOTO BY DWJ)

One thing you need to be aware of with this type of venue is the possibility of inadequate power. I think I've said that power is an issue in every locale we've covered so far, and that's because it is such a critical part of any event. Just be sure that the space has enough power to carry out your mission.

Another issue that often crops up in these spaces is cleanliness. Given the nature of warehouses and hangars, this can be a tall order. A thorough deep cleaning needs to happen prior to the event, so budget sufficient time and money for that.

Suitable restrooms—or the lack thereof—are another thing to keep in mind. These spaces are usually sparse and antiquated, making the restrooms inappropriate for a corporate event. You'll have to bring in restroom trailers unless the venue people can assure you that they have hosted similar-sized affairs and the restrooms were not a problem.

Also, you'll likely have to bring in your own catering kitchen to facilitate any food preparation and serving.

The last things that you need to be aware of in airplane hangars and warehouses are critters—most notably rats and mice, but also birds. It's not the most glamorous thing you'll ever do as an event producer, but you must scout the place for animal droppings and other signs of infestation. If you find evidence of vermin (be prepared; you probably will!), you'll need to bring in a pest control company several weeks before your event to start mitigating that issue.

In airplane hangars, pigeons tend to be the biggest problem. There's nothing worse than pigeon poop on your buffet. There are two solutions you can try:

(a) Send your staff into the building armed with BB guns.
(b) Hire a company to install a special audio device that is imperceptible to humans but that irritates the birds and drives them out.

I don't know about you, but I prefer option (a).

Cruise Ships, Barges, and Yachts

The next topic under Funky Spaces is cruise ships, barges, and yachts. I have had a lot of experience with these vessels and have found that floating structures serve as extraordinary venues for corporate events. They can be breathtaking and exciting, offering experiences that are a complete change of pace for most of your guests.

Cruise ships provide a terrific, unique environment for corporate events because most everyone loves going on a cruise, regardless of the destination. Obviously, the problem is that anybody can book a cruise and get the "cruise" experience. The challenge for an event producer is to actively entertain and celebrate the attendees in a unique way. You can't just let them have a free-for-all at the pool or the bar, or turn them loose on the normal port-of-call tours. You want to create a special feeling, something they can't get on their own. Our clients hire us to produce cruise-ship events that are unique for their specific group of attendees. What we do has to go beyond what the average guest on a cruise ship could get.

Usually, when we produce such an event, the client has chartered the cruise ship for the duration of the cruise. There's no one else on that ship but their attendees. Believe it or not, cruises for corporate events are quite a cost-effective solution. All the food and amenities are included, and some entertainment is already there. I usually choose to upgrade the typical onboard entertainment by replacing it with a different act. Sometimes we'll use the ship's shows and add an extra component or entertainer to them. We always try to create special events and customized diversions for each particular group, above and beyond what the usual cruise guest would experience.

For example, on the day of departure with the typical cruise, guests wait on board for hours without a whole lot to do. It can be pretty boring. But we produced an event with stations set up on the upper decks during boarding. Attendees customized their own flip-flops, goofy hats, and T-shirts with sequins, feathers, paint, and beads all over them. They had a ball. We supplied custom logo mugs that had flashing lights in them for their special "welcome aboard" drink. And when we finally departed, we had an airplane fly over with an enormous banner that had the company's name emblazoned on it. So, from the second those folks got onboard that ship, they knew they were on a unique trip designed especially for them. They felt cared for; they felt like winners. And that was exactly what the client wanted—that the attendees felt special from start to finish. The event started with the right vibe, even before the lines were cast off at the dock.

We try to carry that same level of audience participation and interaction throughout the course of the three, four, or five days we're out at sea. For one cruise event with 2,000 attendees, we designed a treasure hunt that started on the ship and then went from port to port. The guests were given colored bandanas and backpacks that contained treasure maps, treasure-hunting supplies, sunglasses, sunscreen, and bottled water, among other things. Then they chased batches of clues that took them to all the different parts of the ship.

When the ship docked at its first port—the fun-loving city of Key West—the attendees had to take their treasure maps and treasure hunters' backpacks, and work their

CUSTOM TREASURE HUNT EVENT ON CRUISE SHIP FOR CLIENT

way around the island. They hit several museums, bars, and restaurants, where they received gold coins and stamps on their maps. At each stop, they also got a cheeseburger, a margarita, party beads, or something special. Then they boarded the ship again and traveled to Nassau, in the Bahamas, where the treasure hunt continued. And so it went for the duration of the cruise. Their goal was to get their treasure maps stamped and get the right amount of gold coins by the end of the cruise. This would qualify them for a grand-prize drawing on the last day. It was a highly interactive, custom-designed event for a client that wanted to give its people something unique, something that they couldn't get any other way. It was not only fun, but it was also educational.

The highlight of most of our cruise events is our arrival at a private island. This is where we will have set up a big island-style beach party, customized with entertainment and decorations specifically for that group.

Those are just a few of the things you can do to give your clients a unique experience using a cruise event. It's a high-impact, fun, cost-effective way for corporations to entertain.

Having said that, I must also mention that there are a few challenges when producing events at sea. On cruise ships, realize that space is severely limited. This relates to your gear and everything else you'll need for the setup. Every square inch is usually already accounted for, so you have to be highly strategic and selective when planning who and what you're taking onboard the ship. Figure out how long it will take to set up your equipment, and also how much staff you'll bring on board to work in collaboration with the crew.

We produced a shipboard event many years ago, before the cruise lines really started doing a lot of corporate bookings. Back in those days, cruiseship ceilings were extremely low, and everything was boxy and cramped. They weren't anywhere near as nice and as spacious as they are today. We were on a two-week-long, three-event, back-to-back-to-back cruise throughout the Caribbean for a multilevel marketing company. Our gear was stashed in every nook and cranny on that ship. Our stuff was in the closets where the housekeeping crew kept its cleaning equipment. We had stuff in the maintenance room among their gear; we had more items in the supply storeroom and lockers. We had stuff stashed and crammed into all of these places, and then some.

But when we got back to the home port and began to off-load our gear and supplies, we discovered that half of our stuff was missing. It had disappeared into thin air, and no one on the crew seemed to have a clue about what had happened to any of it. We did a little digging around and eventually discovered the truth. The real story was that by the time we had finished the last segment of the event and were steaming back to port, the crew had grown completely sick and tired of our stuff being in their spaces. To vent their frustration, they actually threw a bunch of it overboard! Needless to say, that was an exciting issue to deal with on the back end.

Cruise ships are obviously wonderful venues for the guests, but they present a few challenges for your event production team and the ship's crew. Remember that space is a very territorial thing. Be sensitive to your shipmates' concerns at all times. Don't invade anyone's space without permission, and the odds are good that you won't have to deal with "supplies overboard!" on your next event at sea.

DARREN'S TIP

I always try to get advance permission to commandeer the children's daycare area on board the cruise ship. You can use it for staging, storage, and staffing. Typically there are no kids at these events, and the space will be empty anyway.

Yachts are also awesome spaces in which to do corporate events. They definitely give the attendees a sense of grandeur, opulence, and elegance. That vibe is hard to recreate on anything but a yacht. In my opinion, they are best suited for something like a cocktail cruise that allows for horsd'oeuvres, mixing, and mingling. They are less suited to an event that requires everyone to be in one place on board for any length of time.

Because of the size and choppy configuration of most yachts, your guests will have to be moving around. They will spread out here, there, and everywhere, among various decks, salons, and cabins. Yachts are very accommodating for that type of activity with a guest list of twenty to one hundred people, max. There are a few multilevel yachts that can carry up to three hundred people in some ports, but they aren't much more than floating ballrooms. Still, cruising on the water at night is a wonderful experience at any destination. For a corporate event at which the goal is for your clients to interface or mingle with their attendees (whether they're customers, salespeople, or what have you), face time is very important. A yacht is a great setting for meaningful interaction with small groups.

Yacht owners are usually hypersensitive to outside equipment and gear coming onboard. Due to the space limitations, it's quite difficult to do any type of decorating beyond simple linens, flowers, and LED candles. There are generally strict guidelines for attaching anything to the railings or fixtures on a yacht, and of course, power is fairly limited.

Barges are another interesting venue on which to do a large, corporate event. You have a blank slate—a huge, multitiered, open space on which to create just about anything. You can decorate them, bring dignitaries in on helicopters, and land right on top of the barge—lots of possibilities. Just be aware that the wind can be a big issue on any of these vessels, especially when they're underway, due to the lack of structure to block it.

Tents

Tents have come a long way over the last few decades. Nowadays, they are very contemporary in their architecture and design. Consequently, they have become a popular venue for corporate events where indoor space is not available. The beauty of tent structures is that you can have the feel of an outdoor event with the climate-controlled atmosphere of an indoor site.

There are three main categories of tents:

- **Pole tents**
- **Frame tents**
- **Clear-span tents**

Frame tents are just what they sound like—aluminum-frame tents. These are on the smaller side because they lack structural support. But they do give you an open space with no center poles inside the tent, which is nice.

FRAME TENT (PHOTO BY DWJ)

POLE TENT (PHOTO BY DWJ)

CLEAR-SPAN TENT (PHOTO BY DWJ)

Pole tents are larger. They have poles that go all around the outside, and there are usually multiple center poles going down the middle. These poles can be an issue if you're doing any kind of presentations, because they interrupt the line of sight for your guests. They also take up valuable space in the middle of the tent.

Pole tents and frame tents are the styles that are more readily available at smaller event rental companies. They are also the less expensive choices. I usually limit their use to smaller events where budget is an issue, or housing the catering operation outside of an actual venue.

The best tent is also the most expensive—the clear-span tent. This one is constructed using a big aluminum frame with beams, and no center poles. That allows you to hang decorations, sound, and lighting production equipment inside the tent, which is a huge plus. Clear-span tents have high sidewalls and high ceilings, up to approximately thirty feet. You can even get them now two stories, with glass walls and doors. They are very sturdy structures that can withstand winds up to seventy miles per hour. The clear-span tent is a great option for corporate events at locations that don't already have exactly what you need.

One of the keys to successfully booking tents lies in understanding how to calculate the size of the tent you're going to need. The formula is fairly simple: ten square feet per person for a seated event, plus adequate space for food and beverages, stages, dance floors, and any other equipment or features that will be on the floor. For a stand-up or a reception type of event, you can cut that down to seven square feet per person plus all the equipment needs under the tent. Your tent representative should be able to provide you with this information, and here again, a CAD drawing of your event in the tent will provide you with the best source of information. Don't forget that those tent poles can be tricky and unsightly obstacles to deal with sometimes.

The next consideration in booking tents is determining when you will need flooring. This is a big deal, because the flooring costs can be even higher than the tent rental itself. Whenever your tent is going to be erected on a parking lot or other asphalt or concrete surface, you can probably get away without any flooring, or maybe just carpet on the pavement. If you're on the grass or some other soft surface, you will most likely need some type of flooring if the budget allows. But it also depends on the type of event you're having. If it's an upscale affair, then you should have a floor even if you're on asphalt. If it's a casual, daytime event like a barbecue, you probably don't need to go to the added expense of putting in a floor.

Installing flooring is quite a production. You need a subfloor installed to provide the actual structure. Then you need carpeting or some other decorative layer to cover the whole thing. Like I said, those costs can get up there pretty quickly.

You also have to consider water drainage in and around your proposed tent site. If it rains (or if it has rained prior to the start of your gathering), does water have to flow underneath your tent to get to the drain? I once hosted an event inside a tent that ended up with six inches of water in it. The low spot of the pavement was underneath the center of the tent, and all the water ran to the low spot. It happens. Give careful consideration to drainage when choosing a tent location.

Man, It's Really Hot in Here

If you've ever gone camping, you know that a tent can get hotter than a firecracker inside, especially if you have to drop the sidewalls for privacy or to protect the occupants from rain. If the outside temperature approaches the eighty degrees mark on the day of your event, that tent can become a greenhouse—and your guests are not a bunch of African daisies. Always be aware of the ambient air temperature during the time of year that you're hosting your event; add air-conditioning or heating when the situation calls for it. The most common issue that happens is you may have a breeze blowing through the open tent during setup; then the rain comes, and you have to close the tent walls and suddenly there is no airflow. You should always rent fans during warm weather to increase airflow if you have to close the tent sidewalls. Here again, the costs of temperature control are rather significant, but you gotta do what you gotta do. Just make sure you budget for it.

The final issue with any type of tent installation is the anchoring of the tent to the ground. Have a local inspection company determine where the water lines, sewer lines, cable lines, gas lines, and electrical lines are before the tent company arrives to raise the tent. If they punch a hole in any of those things, you will be the responsible party. So always remember to call first, dig second.

GENERATOR AND AIR-CONDITIONING UNIT (PHOTO BY DWJ)

811 is the universal number to "call before you dig" in the United States. You must call a minimum of two days before your digging is supposed to start so a crew can come out and mark all of the underground stuff for you. But I recommend that you don't cut it that close. Call a week in advance, and cross one more thing off your to-do list.

Remember...

• When booking a museum venue, map out the flow from room to room to make sure there's continuity.

• Be sure there is adequate space for storage, food prep, and logistics.

• Is there sufficient power to fulfill your mission?

• Keep strong winds in mind when planning events on a barge, cruise ship, or yacht.

• Budget for pre-event cleaning and pest control for warehouses and hangars.

• Don't overlook tents as a venue—they have improved greatly in appearance and functionality over the years.

• When calculating tent size, remember: ten square feet per person for seated events and seven square feet for stand-up events, plus all your equipment needs.

• Check out the drainage situation at any proposed tent site.

• Plan to regulate the temperature inside the tent to keep it comfortable for your guests.

• Call first, dig second.

CHAPTER 11

Winning Entertainment

"The human race has one really effective weapon, and that is laughter."

— *Mark Twain*

Entertainment is one of the most crucial elements when producing an event. It requires a thorough understanding of how to match the right entertainer with the right audience. You can definitely lay an egg at an event if you put the wrong act in front of the wrong crowd.

That's why I highly recommend using the services of a good talent agent. I know that event producers are sometimes reluctant to use an agent because they don't want to pay the 20-percent fee. They want to save the dough. But in my opinion, talent agents' services are worth every penny. When you're producing a corporate event with a lot of entertainment components to it, a local entertainment agent can serve as your filter. Whether it's theatrical, dance, name acts, local acts, animals, comedians, stilt walkers, or whatever the case may be, a good agent can distill the quality acts from the not-so-quality acts. Many entertainment acts are trying to move up the ladder from social events or kids' birthday parties to corporate events. There are some real dipsticks out there. Entertainment agents are only going to recommend acts that they know are good, because their reputation is on the line. Reputation is everything in this business, and if word gets around that they provide crappy acts, they will quickly be left out of the referral process.

In addition to helping you weed through the list of potential entertainers, agents will also help you deal with the talent before and during the event. They handle all the communication with the act(s), giving them directions, ensuring that the acts are there on time, and making sure that all of their needs are met. Agents will schedule contracted breaks and all of the other gazillions things that go along with babysitting entertainment.

One item that often gets overlooked is costuming. Anytime you have talent that will be performing in costumes, always have them send you a picture of what they will be wearing. I have seen many a scantily clad dancer or performer sent back to the green room to add more clothing prior to their performance. Typically Corporate America is not hip on too much exposed T and A. Nothing is worse than seeing a performer on stage and realizing that your Brazilian dance troupe is actually Brazilian, wearing fishnets and pasties.

PEOPLE LOVE AUDIENCE PARTICIPATION (PHOTO BY DWJ)

Again, an agent is a service that's worth every penny. Anyone who has ever dealt with artistic entertainers knows that managing those folks is like herding cats. Every entertainer has his own idiosyncrasies, his own quirks, his own needs, his own issues. On event day, you are not going to have the time or the patience to ensure that Mr. Rock Star has a bowl of blue M&Ms in his green room. What a relief it is to have somebody manage that kind of stuff for you—especially when it comes to name acts. They have a lot more demands regarding production needs, green rooms, travel, and so on. You're much better off letting the professionals deal with it.

You would think that bands who tour for a living and do corporate events would know their audience and be on their best behavior, but not always. I'll tell you a story that illustrates what I mean. One particular corporate group—a very conservative company with strict guidelines on proper behavior—had hired one of the most famous rock-and-roll bands in the world to perform on the opening night of their event. This band was probably a little too wild for this group, but they were one of the greatest bands of all time, and the client wanted them.

The band was an hour and a half late getting there due to a mechanical issue with their private jet. My client was not happy about that situation, and even less happy that everybody in the crowd was getting rip-roaring drunk waiting for the band to show up.

When they finally arrived and took the stage, the lead singer shouted out to the crowd, "Hey! Is it okay if we say 'f#*%'?"

No, it was not okay. My client turned as white as a sheet. She wanted to curl up in a ball and hide under the stage—and I wanted to go with her. The only thing that saved me was that I had not actually booked that act.

DARREN'S TIP No matter what type of preventive talks and contractual agreements you have, anything can happen when you're dealing with live entertainment. Get help from a qualified entertainment agent, and you'll minimize the likelihood of embarrassment.

Not every event is worthy of having a name act. When that's the case or when you have a tight budget, local acts can fit the bill quite nicely. Hire dance bands, party bands, aerialists, glassblowers, or body painters. The chances are good that you can find talent in your area. And of course, you can always get that old party standby, the DJ.

DJs are a great resource for entertainment today, but you can never be too vigilant. If you're thinking about booking a particular DJ and you've never seen him or her perform, check to be sure he or she has good, professional equipment that doesn't look or sound like crap. My own personal experience illustrates why I say this. I once hired a DJ that somebody recommended for a function at my house. The guy showed up to do the gig with nothing but a boom box and a microphone. Needless to say, the guy was booted out of there in a hurry. You'd think that after thirty years in this business, I wouldn't be so stupid. I knew better, but I didn't ask the right questions.

Entertainment Riders

Entertainment riders are part of the contractual documents that go with name act performers to outline all the requirements of their production. This includes the sound, lighting, backline, staging, and how everything is supposed to be set up. It will detail what their travel, transportation, and hotel arrangements are. This is where you'll find their requirements for food and beverages, towels, blue M&Ms, bottled water from the South of France, and all the other crazy things that they can think of to ask for in their riders.

I remember one time that I booked a group who was a name act from the sixties and seventies. The two lead singers of that band hated each other so much that in their rider they requested separate flights, separate transfers from the airport, and even rooms on separate hotel floors, so they wouldn't have to run into each other. Fortunately, when they got on stage, they did a great show. They acted like total professionals.

The reality is that some of these riders are unbelievable and it really requires an expert to manage them. Here again, hiring a talent agent who is accustomed to working with these acts can save you a lot of time and trouble. He or she can negotiate and distill the real requirements from the ridiculous.

Live Animal Acts

I have booked all kinds of live animals for events: snakes, parrots, alligators, lions, tigers, and bears—you name it. People love having animals at their events, especially ones that are docile enough to take pictures with. Folks go crazy for that; they line up for miles. I've had big parrots, boa constrictors, and even Florida panthers. We get the panthers out of the cages, and the collared cats sit on the floor with their trainers beside them. Guests get to come up and kneel next to them for a photo; they get to pet them and take a picture with them. For entertainment, it really packs a punch. People want real-life experiences like that. But as much as everybody enjoys having animals around, you have to be completely aware at all times. A lot of things can go wrong, so you have to be ready for everything.

For instance, I used to book lots of lions and tigers to come in and appear at parties. Once we had a huge lion in a cage; the cat would roar and all the guests would freak out. Everybody loved having their pictures taken next to that cage. Well, one time a woman was standing beside the cage, cheesing it up for the camera, and that cat turned around and peed on her—right through the cage bars. It was unbelievable—like a fire hose. Can you imagine getting peed on by a 400-pound lion? It doesn't come out in the first wash, I can tell you that. That poor guest was mortified, and it sure put a damper on her night.

I've had baby alligators pee on the person holding them for a picture. I've had horses come into the ballroom and poop right in the middle of the floor. You have a bag under their tail to catch the poop, but still…it happens.

There's a funny story (well, it's funny now; it wasn't so funny at the time) that happened with another lion. I used to book an ex-lion tamer from Ringling Brothers and Barnum & Bailey who had a bunch of big cats. He had an assortment of jaguars, panthers, African lions, and Bengal tigers—every cat you can imagine. He was like a one-man Siegfried & Roy. He lived with those animals; they were his life. They were very docile and show-friendly. In fact, many of them had been in movies and commercials. He had a large, experienced crew that managed the cats whenever they traveled. I used to take them to events all over the United States. Over the years, I learned which types of events worked well with the cats and which didn't. And I learned about all the things that bothered them.

DARREN AND KAREN WITH JAGUAR
(PHOTO BY DWJ STAFF)

At the close of one particular event, the owner of the cats was short-staffed down at the truck while his crew was bringing more cats down from the hotel, so two of my guys were helping him get the animals into their truck. We were moving a 500-pound African lion in a wheeled, steel cage that weighed another five hundred pounds. As we were pushing the cage up the ramp and into the back of a truck, the lion suddenly ran to one side. The next thing we knew, the cage with the lion in it flipped off the ramp and rolled down a small embankment into a swampy area. Then we had 1,000-pounds of massive, frightened, angry lion and steel cage upside down in a ditch—with only three people to get it out. We needed to get the cage right side up first, but couldn't even touch the bars because the animal was more than a bit angry. When a male African lion is pissed, that roar can be heard for miles. It was the perfect poster for a PETA commercial, right there.

It took us half an hour to calm the lion down and get the cage rolled over and out of the ditch, and up and into that truck. That was one of the scariest moments of my entire life. All I could think of was that cage door busting open and the lion getting loose.

This is the real deal, folks. When something like that happens, safety is the only consideration. Our clients expect—no, they deserve—for us to make sure that they are safe.

DARREN'S TIP   Only book live animal acts that come highly recommended by people you trust. Make sure that every safety precaution is adhered to, proper insurance is provided, and, most notably, the operator has a good track record.

Magicians, Comedians, Hypnotists, and Mentalists

There are many different types of entertainers you can consider for your next event. The old standbys include magicians, comedians, hypnotists, and mentalists. Of those four particular talents, magicians are usually the safest. You typically will not have any issues with them; they're wholesome entertainment. In spite of that, I want to point out that I am not a big fan of having magicians onstage. The acts can be hokey if they're not produced well, with good lighting and proper staging. I've seen many a magic act go south because the audience could easily see what was really happening.

Comedians can be a great addition to your event, but only if you or someone you trust has worked with them before or seen their act from start to finish. Hiring a comedian that you've never seen before can be a bit risky. I have seen many a comic say inappropriate things to audiences, even though they were told to keep it G- or PG-rated, corporate-polished, or something to that effect. It's as if some of them just can't help themselves. Inappropriate comments about gender, race, politics, or sex are determined to come flying out of their mouths.

> **DARREN'S TIP** You cannot rely on a videotape or a webcast of a comedian. They are typically edited to give you a wholesome, generic picture of the performer. You have to see the comedian live to understand the whole gamut of his or her jokes.

Here's how it works. Comedians probe each audience to find out what makes them tick. As soon as they get a reaction on a particular topic, that is where they will continue to work. So if they find they get a lot of laughs from telling jokes about marriage or family or women or gays or politics, they will continue along that track. Once the train starts down that track, you cannot stop it, short of giving them the hook. But by the time you've given them the hook, the damage has already been done. Even if they assure you they understand the boundaries, make sure you reinforce the message about what's acceptable and what's not right before they walk on stage.

Mentalists are the mind readers. They are like glorified magicians, and are usually pretty safe. The shows are all very similar, often with the same or close to the same gags. There must be a mentalist school that they go to, because they all perform the trick of taping coins over their eyes while telling you what your mother's birthday is—a date you have written down and sealed in an envelope that's in your jacket pocket. As with any other performer, just make sure that you or someone you trust has seen them work.

The next set of performers, hypnotists, can be a very scary thing. In my years of booking them, I have seen them get participants to do things that were absolutely hysterical and also shocking. The people involved were either embarrassed afterward or totally pissed about it when they found out what they had done. You have to be very careful with hypnotists to make sure they don't do things that will embarrass your guests.

For instance, I booked a hypnotist once to perform at an event that included a bunch of upper

WHY YOU ALWAYS CHECK COSTUMES BEFORE THE EVENT (PHOTO BY DWJ)

management people. The hypnotist asked for volunteers. Several guys stepped forward, including one particular manager. After about twenty minutes of hypnotizing the group, the hypnotist could tell which ones were in a fringe or twilight hypnosis, and he weeded them out. He was left with about five people on the stage who were absolutely, no doubt, deeply hypnotized. He had them do a series of hilarious things—including a fake strip-tease. The audience members were falling out of their chairs laughing. Then he brought the volunteers out of the hypnosis.

I'm not going to go into the details of the other things the performer had them do, because it really embarrassed one of the men. Out of respect for him, I'm keeping it out of this book. But suffice it to say that when he saw a video of himself doing the things that he was asked to do under hypnosis, he really got upset about it. Some people have a very hard time being the butt of a joke, while others don't.

The moral of the story is this: You're in charge of the event, so you have to be mind-ful. Make sure that the people who volunteer understand exactly what they're in for. You also have to reinforce the message with the hypnotist that you don't want him or her doing anything that will embarrass your guests.

Musical Entertainment

Anytime you're booking musical entertainment for an event, always, *always* be there for the sound check. This is your opportunity to make necessary adjustments. You want to make sure that the music isn't too loud and that they're not playing anything that is inappropriate for your group.

The last thing you want is for the band to open your elegant cocktail reception with "Free Bird," while your client and guests all turn to you with *that* look—you know the one I'm talking about. Your one last chance to eliminate that possibility is at the sound check. There you can go over everything with the band and tell them which sound lev-els are required for the event. That includes music during the dinner and the party after dinner. If it's a dance party and it's all wide-open, so be it. At the sound check you can make sure that everyone's on the same page.

A TYPICAL BACKLINE SET-UP (PHOTO BY DV PIX)

Try to see as many acts in person as you can before you book them. If you can't see acts in advance for whatever reason, rely on a professional entertainment agent. Agents will recommend those that they deem reliable and that they think will fulfill your event goal needs.

The sound check also allows you the opportunity to ensure that you have the right amount of power. If the band starts playing and the breakers pop, you'd probably rather have that happen during a sound check and not during the actual event. Am I right?

Meet and Greet

Whenever you book a name act, always try to arrange a meet and greet. Your VIPs or a limited number of people can then go to the green room and mingle with the performers for pictures and autographs. That's always a great benefit that you should try to negotiate on the front end. It will not happen if you do not prearrange it in the contract. The client is always greatly appreciative when they get the opportunity to go backstage and hang out with the band for a little bit.

One final word on entertainment: no matter how great an act may have been back in its heyday, whether it was the seventies, eighties, nineties, or the 21st century, you need to get current references for that act. A few years ago, I was on the verge of making an offer for the lead singer of a band that had been spectacular in its day. I personally loved that band, so I was excited about the idea of booking the lead singer for an event. I was just about to contract with the guy when something told me to dig a little deeper. I went online and started reading reviews of his recent shows; then I started making some calls. Come to find out, the online reviews and personal references of recent shows were not so favorable. Apparently the guy had had some health issues over the years, and he had lost his edge (and voice). His booking agent did not tell me that. I was so glad that I had taken the time to do my research and avoid a possible disaster.

It is up to you, as the buyer, to conduct your due diligence and find current references for all your acts—including those big-name acts you once loved. The event you save may be your own.

Production

The term "production" consists of all the equipment and services that have to do with sound, lighting, video, and staging. That includes all of the components necessary to support everything from meetings and general sessions to any type of musical or theatrical entertainment. This topic could be a book unto itself. I know just enough about production to know that I should hire people a lot more knowledgeable than I am to handle it.

Take my advice: if you are not well-versed in this category, I highly recommend that you develop a relationship with a production company or a technical director. You need a person who really understands all the intricacies, processes, and requirements. Production is one of the most complicated components of any corporate event. There is so much involved in all of the equipment that you really have to be an expert in it to fully understand all the different elements and technological components.

There is as much variety in the quality and cost of production equipment as there is in cars. You can get a $1,500 car or you can get a $500,000 car—and you get what you pay for. The same is true in sound, lighting, and video. There is a vast array of equipment in this category. This is important if you have a name act playing your event. They may have a rider specifying the exact audio, lighting, and staging they want. You have to be capable of providing it. The band has to know that when they get to your gig, they will not have any inferior equipment. Substandard equipment will make the musicians sound bad, which hurts their reputation and jeopardizes their livelihood. That's why the riders for these acts are as specific as they are.

By far, the single most important component in production is audio. The lighting can be mediocre and it won't ruin a show. The same goes with the stage set. But if the audio is bad—if it's cracking and popping, if there's squealing, if the sound board isn't up to date or adequate—it will wreck the show faster than anything else. It's very likely that the band will not even get on stage to perform.

BACK STAGE VIDEO CITY (PHOTO BY DWJ)

FLYING THE LIGHTING (PHOTO BY DV PIX)

I have developed relationships with several production companies and professionals. I can rely on their expertise to make sure that every one of those production elements is done in a professional manner. These people deal with the power, the rigging, the setup, the crews, the union labor, the trucking, and all of the other stuff specified in most event and entertainment riders. Whether you have a production company that provides all that gear or an individual technical director who can source all that equipment for you, you need that kind of professional expertise. Some production companies specialize just in audio, others in lighting, others in staging, and still others in video only. Then there are the full-service companies that provide a total one-stop shop. It really just depends on your degree of necessity.

Here again, power comes back into play. You'll probably have very heavy, specific power requirements to support that level of sound, lighting, and video equipment. If a venue doesn't have it, you can look to your production company to source it for you or give you exactly what you need. These guys are life- and sanity-savers.

The importance of hiring a top-flight production company cannot be overemphasized.

Wow Factors

"Wow" factors are anything that you use or hire to create a special effect or a big impact for an event. They can be used to open an event, to highlight the introduction of a VIP, or as a way to close an event. There are lots of really cool techniques for doing this, including pyrotechnics, illusions, wish lanterns, lasers, and confetti.

Outdoor Fireworks

Obviously, a fireworks show is a very common way to close or highlight an event, most notably a nighttime event. Fireworks are awesome for outdoor events where you have big spaces, big crowds, and a budget that allows you to pay for it. Actually, fireworks are now quite reasonable in price. In just about any city, you can get a decent fireworks show for $3,000 to $10,000.

BIG WOW (PHOTO BY DWJ)

A funny (in hindsight) story about fireworks comes from one of the Olympic Games. I don't recall which Olympics it was, but the event producer was using a combination of white doves and fireworks for either the opening or closing ceremony. The white doves were released and were circling the stadium. They were making their second or third lap when the fireworks started going off. The noise literally scared the crap out of those birds. It was like a rainstorm of bird poop coming down on all those people in the stadium.

Whenever you're using fireworks, be aware that animals—big, small, and in between—are very afraid of them. Be sensitive to that, and avoid potential problems for the animals and for your guests.

Speaking of birds, doing some type of white dove release is a great feature or enhancement for any outdoor event, especially something that's of a sentimental nature. The people who do those releases typically do a beautiful job, and they're reasonably priced as well.

Chinese Wish Lanterns

A fairly new practice in our country is the use of Chinese sky or wish lanterns. These are paper lanterns that have a small cradle for a candle. You open the shade and place the lit candle inside on the cradle. The heat from the candle will create the same effect as a hot-air balloon. The heat actually lifts the lantern into the sky, and it travels as far as it can until the candle burns out. When you release the lantern to fly, you are supposed to make a wish.

COOL WOW FACTOR (PHOTO BY DWJ)

The lanterns can be used for any type of celebration, from a corporate event to a wedding. It looks absolutely awesome when a hundred of them rise into the night sky in unison. It's especially effective at a waterfront location. The lanterns also come in a biodegradable option, so that when they land, they will not hurt the environment. You must be very diligent in determining their flight path so that they don't catch anything on fire when they land. That's why I only use them over water. It is a great look that everyone can participate in, and it's inexpensive, like $5 to $15 each depending on the size.

Confetti Cannons and Balloons

Confetti cannons are air-pressurized tubes that shoot confetti and streamers out over the heads of your guests. They create a lot of fun for people. You can use them as an extra enhancement for stages, event openings, closings, or any kind of celebration, really. You can get cannons small enough to operate within a ballroom or big enough to cover a large space. There are monster confetti cannons on wheels that can blow an incredible amount of confetti around. They make it look like a Wall Street ticker-tape parade, or some massive celebration in a sports venue like a Super Bowl. Very impressive!

Another unique item is the confetti balloon. These are filled with air and confetti and then hung from the ceiling of a ballroom or other indoor venue. To the untrained

CONFETTI CANON (PHOTO BY DWJ)

eye, they look exactly like big, normal balloons that are attached to the ceiling. But here's the kicker: there's a battery-powered electrical unit attached to the balloon. You have a remote control device. At the exact moment that you want the balloons to explode, you hit the button on the remote, which sends a signal to the battery-powered unit. A little electrical charge shoots out of the unit and pops the balloon, releasing all the confetti to sprinkle down over the space. It's a very cool effect that I actually used myself on one occasion.

I did run into a little issue that one time, though. I was at a Ritz-Carlton hotel doing an awards dinner for a corporate client. We had put confetti balloons up on the ceiling, along with their little battery-powered units. At the close of the evening, at the given time, we hit the remote control, and all the balloons popped on cue. But one of the balloons up by the stage had a big piece of the latex rubber still hanging on it. The battery-powered unit kept firing off instead of stopping when it was supposed to, and that caught the dangling piece of balloon on fire.

Then I had a small burning balloon the size of a credit card attached to the ceiling of the Ritz-Carlton. It was about eighteen feet up in the air, and no ladder was readily accessible. The fire ended up setting off the smoke alarms in the ballroom, and everybody had to be evacuated. It took us about ten minutes of scrambling to find a ladder that would reach the balloon. In the meantime, the balloon continued to burn, blackening the ceiling, and the latex was melting and dripping on the carpet. So I had two issues to deal with at the Ritz-Carlton that night: a black sooty ceiling from the fire, and a carpet that was a bit of a mess thanks to dripping rubber.

Note to self: I'm not sure I want to ever use those confetti balloons again. As a matter of fact, I haven't used them since that night. Come to think of it, I haven't even seen them around lately. All in all, if a client asks you about using confetti balloons, steer them in another direction—or have a fire extinguisher handy.

Keep in mind that anytime you use confetti cannons, confetti balloons, or confetti in any capacity, it will have an effect on the ground surface. If you are dropping confetti on a hard surface like a dance floor or concrete, it will become very slippery, and people could slip and hurt themselves. If you can, try to have workers ready with blowers or brooms to sweep it up right after the drop. If it's on carpet, there is no issue.

Illusions

When one thinks of illusions or illusionists, the first name that usually pops up is David Copperfield. We've seen him walk through the Great Wall of China, make cars with people inside disappear, and even make 747 airplanes appear right in front of our eyes. There are many not-as-famous professional illusionists who can create the same type of dramatic appearance at your show or event. You can make top management or celebrity guests suddenly appear sitting atop a Harley or even inside a car; I mean make the vehicle or the Harley and person appear, not just the person. Illusionists can be used for any type of powerful product reveal or meeting opener. There is a significant production requirement to fulfill these types of acts, but they are definitely dramatic and create a *real wow!*

Indoor Pyro and Fireworks

With indoor pyro and fireworks, you have loud explosions, you have smoke, and you have fire in these elements that are made specifically for indoor events. Obviously, you need to have permits for these items.

One lesson I learned the hard way is to be very careful about how much indoor pyrotechnics you use in a given space. We produced an event one time using a big theatrical dance troupe. Toward the close of the event, we had a grand finale that was supposed to include indoor pyro. This particular pyrotechnics company wanted to show us what a great job it could do, so it really beefed up the show. Usually when somebody gives you something extra, you think of that as being a good thing. In this case, it was too much of a good thing. The pyro created so much smoke in the ballroom that the air system could not ventilate it. Smoke got into the public spaces of the building, which set off alarms and strobes for the entire twenty-story hotel at 11 p.m. on a Saturday night. The fire department came, and the place was completely evacuated. It was not a pretty sight.

So, anytime you're going to use indoor pyro, I highly recommend that you use just enough to accomplish your goal. Think of it only as an enhancement for your grand finale—not as the be-all and end-all. Remember, in this case, less is more.

Lasers

If you're looking for something with a little more impact, lasers are a great feature—indoors or outdoors. They are rather expensive and need to be scripted with music for best effect, so they require professional guidance to properly use them. They are great for opening an act or in conjunction with fireworks.

LASERS (PHOTO BY DWJ)

If you're ever going to use lasers, be aware that you need a lot of smoke. The smoke is what allows you to see the striking beam patterns of the lasers. The smoke required for outdoor laser shows is typically generated by fireworks. There are specific fireworks that generate extra smoke for use in conjunction with lasers. Therefore, if your event is outdoors, wind could be an issue for both the fireworks and the smoke. When it's windy, it's harder to control the smoke. You may still be able to see the lasers being drawn or etched on a surface, but to get the full effect, you need the combination of lasers and regulated smoke. That combination really creates the wow factor. For that reason, lasers work a little bit better inside, in a controlled environment, where you can use a water based haze to get the full effect.

CO2 Cannon

The final wow factor is the CO2 cannon. These are great, loud special effects that you can use on stages to introduce VIPs, do closings, or whatnot. They blow a big, loud cloud of carbon dioxide and make a massive boom that definitely gets everyone's attention. They are great to use—and no mess.

Remember...

- Develop a relationship with a good entertainment agent. He or she will save you a lot of time and embarrassment.

- Make sure your live animal acts come with recommendations you can trust.

- Same with comedians; be sure their brand of humor fits the occasion and the crowd.

- Show up for all sound checks.

- Always try to arrange a meet and greet; your clients will love it.

- Check current references and reviews for all acts, even big-name acts.

- Call in a professional production company or technical director to help you navigate the production minefield.

- With production equipment, you get what you pay for.

- Audio is the most critical component of production.

- Fireworks scare animals.

- Lasers need smoke to be really effective; therefore, they're better-suited for controlled environments.

- Use indoor pyro sparingly.

- Illusionists can create dramatic openings for product reveals and guest appearances.

Chapter 12

Last Call

"The secret to creativity is knowing how to hide your sources."

– Albert Einstein

The business of corporate event production is an extremely exciting and gratifying career. It is not well suited for people who cannot organize, deal with stress or pressure, or think fast on their feet. As I stated previously, I love the pressure and adrenaline rush that comes with being on-site and making it all happen, day in and day out.

There are very few jobs or careers in this world that can provide constant variety, freedom to express your creativity, and the ability for instant gratification as you witness the successful event that you have just produced unfold. This is one of those careers.

Embrace it and enjoy the ride.

It has been amazing to see the great evolution of the event industry over the last thirty years, and to see how it continues to grow. I am very thankful that this once mom-and-pop business has blossomed into such a meaningful and significant international industry. Corporations continue to move more marketing dollars into live events than ever before as they try to touch consumers one by one.

I am sure that companies and individual event producers probably have a bunch of really cool online forms and lots of fancy online tools that they use when producing an event. That's great for them, and they are probably very efficient, but I'm old-school; I freely admit it. I've been using the same forms and systems for decades for one simple reason: because they work for me.

There's no need for you to reinvent the wheel unless you want to. In the pages that follow, I present some of the forms I most commonly use to manage the nuts and bolts of stuff like confidentiality agreements, scheduling, and the like. Feel free to modify them to suit your needs. As far as the legal documents go, I strongly suggest having your own legal counsel create contracts and agreements that are pertinent and binding in your state. The ones provided in the Appendix are for reference only and are not intended to be legally binding documents.

APPENDIX: FORMS THAT MAY HELP

CONFIDENTIALITY AND NONDISCLOSURE AGREEMENT

This Agreement is made this _____ day of _____, 20____, by and between _____ ("Company") and _____("Vendor" or "Vendors") (Company and Vendors are each a "Party" and collectively the "Parties"). In consideration of the mutual undertakings contained herein, the Parties agree as follows:

CONFIDENTIALITY

1. Confidential Information. The Parties agree that the information from any source concerning any activities, terms, conditions, structure, business, finances, and management of the Company and the Company's Clients, as well as their existing and proposed business activities and endeavors, are of a proprietary and confidential nature ("Confidential Information"). Confidential information is, and shall remain, the exclusive property of the Company. Each Party shall treat and maintain all such Confidential Information as confidential, whether or not designated as such. Vendor and Vendor's Employees shall hold in a fiduciary capacity for the benefit of Company all Confidential Information, along with any inventions, discoveries, concepts, ideas, improvements, or know-how discovered or developed by Company, solely or jointly with other Companies, during the term of this Agreement, which may be directly or indirectly useful in or related to the business of Company or its affiliates. The Confidential Information may be used only as permitted by the Agreement and may not, under any circumstances, be released to any other person, entity, or the public without the prior written consent of the Company. Notwithstanding the foregoing, such Confidential Information may be released if required under Court Order, so long as reasonable efforts are made to narrow the scope of the disclosure.

2. Nondisclosure. Each Party shall treat and maintain all such Confidential Information as confidential, whether or not designated as such. The Confidential Informa-

tion may be used only as permitted by the Agreement and may not, under any circumstances, be released to any other person, entity, or the public without the prior written
consent of the Company. Notwithstanding the foregoing, such Confidential Information may be released if required under Court Order, so long as reasonable efforts are
made to narrow the scope of the disclosure. Vendors will not, during or after the term
of this agreement, directly or indirectly, use, disseminate, or disclose to any person,
firm, or other business entity for any purpose whatsoever, any trade secrets, intellectual
property, or information not generally known in the industry in which Company is or
may be engaged which was disclosed to Vendor or known by Vendor as a consequence
of or through Company's relationship with Vendor. This includes information regarding Company's products, processes, customers, services, suppliers, and related matters,
and also includes information relating to research, development, inventions, manufacturing, purchasing, accounting, engineering, marketing, merchandising, and selling.

3. Permitted Disclosures. Parties may reveal the Confidential Information as strict-
ly necessary for legal, accounting, and tax advice, but must seek the written permission
of the Company prior to revealing the Confidential Information. Managers of the
Company will be permitted to disclose such Confidential Information as they believe
is in the best interests of the Company.

REMEDIES ON BREACH

1. Injunctive Relief. Vendor agrees that violating this agreement at any time, including during litigation, will produce severe damage and injury to Company. In the
event of the breach of, or threatened breach by Vendor of this agreement, Company
shall be entitled to seek injunctive relief, without bond, both preliminary and perma-
nent, enjoining and restraining such breach or threatened breach. Such remedies shall
be in addition to all other remedies available to Company in law or in equity, including but not limited to, Company's right to recover from Vendor any and all damages
that may be sustained as a result of Vendor's breach.

2. Liquidated Damages. Vendor agrees that, in the event of violation by Vendor of
this agreement, Vendor will pay as liquidated damages to Company the sum of $___.__
per day, for each day or part thereof that Vendor continues to breach the agreement.
Further, as liquidated damages, if Vendor, without written consent of Company fails
to comply with any provisions of this agreement, Vendor's right to any commissions
or bonus to which Vendor would otherwise be entitled shall terminate and Company's
obligation to make any such payment shall cease. It is recognized and agreed that
damages in such event are difficult to ascertain, though great and irreparable, and that
this agreement with respect to liquidated damages shall in no event prevent Company
from obtaining injunctive relief.

3. Agreement Survives Termination. All rights of the parties pursuant to this agreement shall survive any termination or cessation of Vendor's business relationship with Company.

4. Choice of Law and Venue. The validity, interpretation, and performance of this agreement shall be controlled by and construed under the laws of the State of _____. Both parties agree that any objections to venue be waived, and that venue shall be in the Circuit Court for _____.

5. Attorney's Fees. If an attorney shall be retained to interpret or enforce the provisions of this agreement, the prevailing party shall be entitled to reasonable attorney's fees, including any such fees set by the trial or appellate court upon trial or appeal.

6. Notice. All notices or other communications required or permitted to be made or given under this Agreement, by one Party to any other Party, shall be in writing and shall be deemed to have been given: (1) when hand delivered; (2) on the third (3rd) business day after the day of deposit in the United States mail when sent by certified mail, postage prepaid, and return receipt requested; (3) on the next business day if by overnight mail; or (4) when sent by fax or e-mail upon confirmation of receipt. Such notice shall be sent to the address set forth below, or to the fax number or e-mail address of the Party:

Company:
   Address
   Address

Vendors:
   Name
   Address
   Address

7. Severability. Each of the provisions of this agreement shall be enforceable independently of any other provision of this agreement and independent of any other claim or cause of action.

8. Waiver. No failure or delay by either Party hereto in exercising any right, power, or privilege hereunder shall operate as a waiver thereof, nor shall any single or partial exercise thereof preclude any other future exercise of any right, power, or privilege.

9. Counterparts. This Agreement may be executed in multiple identical counterparts (with one Party signing certain counterparts and the other Party signing other counterparts) or with detachable signature pages, which shall be construed together and shall be effective if all executed in one, unified document. When all counter-

parts of this Agreement have been signed by the Parties, it shall constitute a binding agreement. This Agreement shall become effective as of the date the last Party to the Agreement signs hereto. A facsimile or electronic scan shall constitute delivery for all purposes.

IN WITNESS WHEREOF, the parties hereto have set their hands and seals on the day and year first above written.

COMPANY   VENDOR

_____   _____

This document is being presented as a reference and not intended to be used as a legally binding document. Please have your legal counsel provide one for your area or state.

EVENT TIMELINE FORM

DARREN // JOHNSON
PRODUCTIONS
Killer Live Events

Opening Night Timeline – "GAME ON"

TIME	DATE	EVENT	LOCATION	GREEN ROOM STAFF	PARKING VALIDATIONS
8AM-6PM		Load-In	BC Ballroom	Set-by 5:30PM	
7:30PM		Doors Open, Bars, Casino Games, Slots	BC	65	65
		Photo Booths, Flip-books	BC Foyer		
		DJ Music-"On the Double"			
		Super Trivia-Continuous	Main Stage		
			LoungeArea	2	2
8:15PM		Horse Race/Kiosk Betting			
8:30PM		"On the Double"	Big Screens	3	3
9:15PM		Boxing Matches/Kiosk Betting	Main Stage	2	2
9:30PM		"On the Double"	Big Screens		
10:15PM		Car Races/Kiosk Betting	Main Stage		
10:30 PM		Last Bets at Casino-Cash-in	Big Screens		
10:45 PM		Auction begins	BC		
11:00 PM		Event Concludes	Main Stage		
Total				72	72

Green Room- to be set by 5:30PM with 5 rounds of 10
Beverages to include water, coffee, and sodas
Hand towels
3 lined trash cans
Parking validation for 72

EVENT LOAD-IN SCHEDULE

Killer Live Events

LA Load-In Schedule

Event Name_____   On Site-Crew: Darren Johnson- Producer
Convention Center West Hall B   Name-Lead
2/1-2/5/2012   Name-Crew
Load-in Schedule V5   Name-Crew
                                            Name-Crew
                                            Name-Crew

L.A. Schedule Recap

DATE	TIME	FUNCTION	LOCATION
Wednesday, February 1, 2012	0700-1500	Crew Travel to LA	Hall B
	1700-1900	Crew Training	
			Hall B
Thursday, February 2, 2012	0700-2000	Load-In	Loading Dock
Friday, February 3, 2012	0800-1900	Show Day 1	Hall B
Saturday, February 4, 2012	0800-1900	Show Day 2	Hall B
	1900-2400	Load-out	Hall B
Sunday, February 5, 2012	0600-1900	Crew Travel Home	
		Truck to ATL	

Load-In Detail

DATE	TIME	FUNCTION	CONTACT PERSON	LOCATION
2/2/2012	0700	LACC space ready for Load-in	Name-Phone#	Hall B
		DWJP Crew Call/Load-in Meeting	Darren Johnson	Hall B
		Truck in	Name&#	Loading Dock
		Mark Floor	Name &#	Hall B
		Set-up Radios/Pagers	Name &#	Hall B
	0730	Local Crew Call	Name &#	Hall B
		House Crew Call (IT, Phone, Electric)	Name &#	
		AV Crew call	Name &#	
		Load-in		
		Central Park Decor	Name +2 locals	
		Booths	Name + 2 locals	
		Viewing centers	Name + 4 locals	

Load-In Detail (con't)

DATE	TIME	FUNCTION	CONTACT PERSON	LOCATION
2/2/2012	0800	Rental co. delivers 150 6'x30" tables		Hall B
	0930	Tables Dropped/linens on	Name + 2 locals	
	1200	Lunch	All	
	1300	Resume Load-in		
		Education/Kids Zone	Name +3 locals	
		Tents/Arches	Name + 3 locals	
		Umbrella Tables/Carts/Misc. Décor	Name + 2 locals	
	1500	Foliage delivered/set	Plant Co. &#	
	1700	Local crew cut		
	2000	DWJP crew cut- Show ready		
		LACC to clean/refresh room		Hall B

Show Days Detail

DATE	TIME	FUNCTION	CONTACT PERSON	LOCATION
2/3-4/2012	800	DWJP Crew Call		Hall B
		Check and prepare all systems		
	1000	Show Floor Opens		Hall B
		Lunch on rotation		TBD
	1700-1830	Dinner on rotation		TBD
	1900	Show floor closes		Hall B

Note: Cleaning crew to clean, bus, and refresh throughout entire show days

Load-Out Detail

DATE	TIME	FUNCTION	CONTACT PERSON	LOCATION
2/4/2012	1900	Truck In	Driver	Hall B
		DWJP Crew		
		Local Labor (16)		
		Foliage Pickup		
		House Electric remove gear		
		Cleaning Crew		
		IT/AV-Remove gear		
		Rental Co. PU tables		Hall B
		Local labor cut		
		DWJP Crew cut		

EVENT POWER & RIGGING SCHEDULE

Program Load-In Schedule

Sales Conference
Hotel:
Date:
Load-in Schedule V1

VIP CLUB:	Wednesday, February 29
Location:	Ballroom
Pax:	350
Set-up:	8am
Event Time:	6:00pm -11:00pm

DESCRIPTION	TRUCK QTY	LOAD-IN	LOAD-OUT	POWER (20 AMPS)	RIGGING
Drape	1	8am	11pm		N/A
Décor	1	9am	11pm	12	
Tables/chairs	2	10am	11pm		
Linen	1	1pm	11pm		
Florals	1	2pm	11pm		

OPENING NIGHT:	Thursday, March 1
Location:	Ballroom
Pax:	1500
Set-up:	7am
Event Time:	7:30pm-11:00pm

DESCRIPTION	TRUCK QTY	LOAD-IN	LOAD-OUT	POWER (20 AMPS)	RIGGING
Horse racing	1	7am	11:30 pm	4	
Seating Platform	1	7am	11:30pm		
Décor	1	9am	11:30pm		N/A
Furniture	2	10am	11:30pm		
Casino/Slots	1	Noon	11:30pm	8	
Linens	1	1pm	11:30pm		

PARTY FOR THE SENSES:	Friday, March 2
Location:	Ballroom
Pax:	1500
Set-up:	6am
Event Time:	7:00pm-11:00pm

DESCRIPTION	ROOM	TRUCK QTY	LOAD-IN	LOAD-OUT	POWER (20 AMPS)	RIGGING
Barcelona	**1-3**					
Hotel stage/Dance floor		1	6am	11:30pm		
Décor		1	8am	11:30pm	3	

PARTY FOR THE SENSES:		Friday, March 2 (CON'T)				
DESCRIPTION	ROOM	TRUCK QTY	LOAD-IN	LOAD-OUT	POWER (20 AMPS)	RIGGING
Barcelona	**1-3**					
Hotel stage/dance floor			6am	11:30pm		
Décor		1	8am	11:30pm	3	
Bar		1	9am	11:30pm	1	
Foliage		1	1pm	11:30pm		
Up-lighting			2pm	11:30pm	4	
Furniture		2	10am	11:30pm		
Linens/barstools		1	1pm	11:30pm		
Band		1	4pm	11:30pm	3	
Stage lighting			1pm	11:30pm	6	
Pulse	**4-9**					
Décor		1	Noon	11:30pm		
Lounge seating		1	Noon	11:30pm		
Hotel dance floor			Noon	11:30pm		
Big Bad Bar with backbar			Noon	11:30pm	2	
Linens/barstools		1	2pm	11:30pm		
Dance floor cover		1	1pm	11:30pm		
VJ			4pm	11:30pm		
Up-lighting			3pm	11:30pm	6	
The Bubble Room Lounge	**10-12**					
Hotel stage 16'x24'			6am	11:30pm		
Décor			8am	11:30pm		
Bars		1	10am	11:30pm		
Floral		1	4pm	11:30pm		
Lounge furniture		1	9am	11:30pm		
Ceiling décor/rigger		1	1pm	11:30pm		
Aerialist/rigger			3pm	11:30pm		
Violectric 6pc			4pm	11:30pm	4	
Stage lighting		1		11:30pm		
Up-lighting		1	3pm	11:30pm	4	
Soul Train	**A-F**					
Hotel stage-18'x24'x32"			6am	11:30pm		
Hotel dance floor-(2)			6am	11:30pm		
12'x18'			9am	11:30pm		
Décor		1	10am	11:30pm	4	
Ceiling décor			10am	11:30pm		In-3pm
Lighted dance floor		1	4pm	11:30pm	2	Out-11:30pm
Band/stage lighting		1	1pm	11:30pm	6	
Linens		1	2pm	11:30pm		
Up-lighting				11:30pm	4	

FINAL NIGHT:	Saturday, March 3
Location:	Ballroom
Pax:	1500
Set-up:	Noon
Event Time:	7:00pm -11:00pm

DESCRIPTION	ROOM	TRUCK QTY	LOAD-IN	LOAD-OUT	POWER (20 AMPS)	RIGGING
Hotel stage/dance floor	BC	2	1pm	11pm		N/A
Décor	BC	1	4pm			

Event Speak: Terms and Lingo

"We are driven by five genetic needs: survival, love and belonging, power, freedom, and fun."

– William Glasser

Every industry has its own unique language, and the event industry is no exception. This list is for those people charged with putting on events—or people who just want to learn some weird stuff.

Action station: This term refers to a food function whereby the catering operation provides a chef-attended station, like a carving station (roast beef, ham, turkey, etc.), or a pasta station, where a chef prepares your order while you wait or cooks in large batches as guests move through the line. There is action at the food station.

Additional insured: This is a term used on a company's general liability policy whereby they list additional entities to be covered on their existing general liability policy.

Amps: Used to power equipment, speakers, lighting, or instruments. Also a measurement of electrical current (amperes).

Audio: Sound or sound equipment.

AV; Audiovisual: The equipment and service that includes sound, lighting, video, and staffing to be used for an event or production.

Back-of-the-house: This typically refers to the service areas where the venue employees work, such as the kitchen, engineering, and storage areas.

Backbar: The table or unit behind the bar that holds glassware or beverages.

Backdrop: A drape or piece of scenery used on a stage to highlight a speaker or entertainer. A backdrop is used to create a focal point or a canvas for lighting effects.

Backline: This is the equipment a band uses to perform. It is their keyboards, drums, amps, pianos, and so on. When hiring a name act, you typically have to provide this equipment. All the backline details are clearly spelled out in the band's rider.

Backstage: Behind the stage or stage backdrop.

Belly bars: Forty-two-inch-tall cocktail tables, typically thirty or thirty-six inches in diameter; also known as tallboys.

Boneyard: The location where cases, dollies, carts, and equipment are stored when they're not being used during an event. It is usually a designated area either backstage or in a hidden space in the venue, close to where the event is staged to allow easy access.

Boxed skirting: A floor-length tablecloth for rectangular banquet tables that hangs straight down with no pleats. It is much cleaner and more contemporary-looking than a typical tablecloth skirting with pleats.

Cabling: Typically used to supply power from the source to whatever requires the power. Used extensively in production to supply power to amps, dimmer racks, speakers, controls, and so on. Proper management of cabling is required to not only avoid an eyesore, but also to minimize any safety issues, such as tripping or egress hazards.

CAD: Computer-aided drawing; CADs are used to create a floor plan of exactly where everything is to be placed in the event space. CADs are required for most public venues and are submitted to fire marshals and local authorities for approval to ensure proper spacing for egress and emergency services. They also indicate placement for crews bringing in components of the event. Also referred to as a floor plan.

Call time: The hour at which your crew, staff, or talent are to be at a specified location.

Carpet runner: Used to create a special walkway for guests or award winners. White and red are typically used because they photograph the best and are associated with Hollywood-type award ceremonies.

Cash bar: A bar where guests pay for their own beverages.

Chair cover: A fabric cover designed to go over a banquet, Chivari, or folding chair. They come in many different styles and fabrics. They can also be accented with a sash, chair band, flowers, feathers, or rhinestones.

Chivari: A type of wooden chair that is typically a rental item. It comes with a seat cushion and many cover options. Used for more upscale and elegant events.

Container: This one has two entirely different meanings in the event industry. The first one is what a florist puts the flowers into for an arrangement. The second definition is the big twenty- to fifty-three-foot metal box that is used to transport goods on ships and trucks. Rarely used together.

Corkage fee: The amount you pay to bring your own wine into an establishment. Many venues allow you to bring in your own wine, and they charge usually a flat fee ranging from $5 to $25 per bottle.

Décor: Anything used to enhance the look or feel of an event space. It includes items such as props, furniture, flowers, linens, plants, and more.

Distro (Distribution): Referred to as the power distribution needed to supply power to specific equipment locations. This distribution equipment typically consists of boxes that host multiple breakers and the cabling needed to deliver the power to the specific location.

Drayage: Delivery of goods to the booth from the receiving dock, storage of empty crates and extra products at a warehouse on-site or close by, and transfer of goods from the booth to the receiving dock and loading them back onto the carrier. Drayage is usually charged at convention centers for trade shows.

Egress: The act of going or coming. Emergency services refer to it as the ability for guests to leave a venue in case of an emergency.

Engineering: The employees at a venue who are responsible for all of the services such as electrical, plumbing, HVAC (air-conditioning), and sprinklers.

Entertainment: Entertainment is categorized in different groups. Typically those groups are local, name, interactive, theatrical, strolling, or atmospheric. Each has a specific use, function, and style.

F&B: Food and beverage.

Fly the gear: The term that refers to hanging or suspending the production equipment, such as audio, lighting, and video. This can only be done with the assistance of a certified rigger or rigging company.

Foliage: Plants, trees, shrubs, and potted flowers.

Foo-Foo: Décor considered soft goods, such as fabrics, flowers, and accent items.

Forklift: An electric- or propane-powered vehicle with long steel forks that is used to load and off-load trucks. Forklifts work best when loading and off-loading equipment on pallets.

Generator: A standalone, gas- or diesel-powered unit that can generate power for equipment. Generators come in all sizes, based on the amount of electrical service required. The larger generators are now referred to as "quiet diesel" because they are less intrusive from a noise standpoint.

Gobo: A glass or metal template used in lighting to project a logo, statement, or image. The lighting fixture that houses the gobo is called a leko.

Grats: Gratuity; a percentage of the food and beverage service that goes to the service and wait staff. This is added to any F&B purchase and ranges from eighteen to twenty-four percent.

Green Room: A secluded private space where your entertainers can get ready, sit, and relax prior to and after their performance.

Hold: The term for reserving an act, a venue, or a piece of equipment. This is done during the planning phase of the event. You place a hold on the item, venue, or act to ensure first right of refusal in case someone else is inquiring about the same item as you and also to lock in the quoted price.

Hosted bar: A bar that the client pays for, allowing invited guests to drink for free.

IT/Internet Technology: The person or persons in a venue or at an event who are responsible for providing Internet connectivity to the appropriate users.

Labor: The group of people hired to assist with setup, takedown, or operations of an event.

Lighting: Any lighting that is used to illuminate or enhance a specific object or area, or to create an atmosphere or vibe. Lighting is usually broken into various subcategories such as stage lighting (used on the stage for speakers and entertainment), décor lighting (used to enhance and illuminate décor in the event space), and house lighting (lights that are permanently affixed in the venue).

Linens: Typically refers to the tablecloths that go on top of tables. Can also refer to the collective group of items that is comprised of tablecloths, napkins, and chair covers.

Load-In/Load-Out: The time during which you load into a venue and the time you load out of the venue. Usually you give vendors a specific time to do these, ensuring that there is an orderly process to the scheduling.

Loading dock: The location, usually in the rear or side of the venue, where large trucks back up to unload. The term "dock" means that it is elevated to match up with the same height as a tractor-trailer or box truck–type vehicle. If a venue does not have a loading dock, you must have a vehicle with either a liftgate or a forklift to get the stuff out of the truck and lower it to the ground.

Logistics: All of the details and items to be planned and managed to produce an event.

Lounge seating: Today, more and more events are using lounge-type environments. They allow employees, management, consumers, or attendees to sit in a casual, relaxed atmosphere like a living room or Starbucks-type setting. Lounge seating can be traditional sofas, love seats, and chairs, as well as smaller cocktail tables and chairs. You can usually get the cocktail tables and chairs from the venue versus having to rent them from an outside vendor. I like mixing both components to get the best value, as the site stuff is usually free and can be covered rather inexpensively.

Mark (or Spike) the floor: This term refers to putting white tape down in premeasured locations to indicate where certain equipment and stages are to be placed. On the stage, a spike mark is used to mark where individuals should stand.

Overlay: The smaller 90-inch tablecloth that goes over a longer 120- or 130-inch tablecloth. Used as an accent to the under cloth or underlay.

P&D (Pipe and Drape): Pipe is the aluminum hardware used to hang fabric drape. Pipe is used when the drape needs to be ground supported. P&D is used for trade show–type booths, masking or hiding areas not to be viewed by the public or audience. Pipe and drape is commonly used as a stage backdrop or to outline a room to create a different look or environment. The drape comes in many different colors and fabrics.

Pallet: A wood or plastic platform that equipment is stacked or loaded onto. These platforms are elevated to allow a pallet jack or forklift to slide the forks underneath for ease of movement or loading and unloading into a truck. Pallets can hold a large amount of weight in a very small footprint.

Pallet jack: The piece of equipment used to move pallets around. The pallet jack is not powered and is manually operated.

Place cards: A card with the guest's name on it, indicating where each person is to sit at a table.

Plus–Plus: This is a term that refers to the purchase of F&B; it means that in addition to the cost of the F&B, you must add the gratuity and local sales tax. Gratuity is typically taxed, as well.

Power: The electrical service needed to run any equipment. When ordering power at a location, it is typically measured in amps and circuits. The usual circuit is a fifteen- or twenty-amp circuit. For larger production equipment (such as sound, lighting, and video), a power order could include a two hundred-amp three-phase order for the lighting, and a one hundred-amp three-phase order for the sound. Never put both sound and lighting on the same power source—unless you enjoy the loud humming that lighting causes in a sound system.

Premium bar: There are three types of bars you encounter when ordering beverage service for an event: House, Standard, and Call/Premium. The House is made up of the cheapest brands, the Standard is the medium-priced brands, and the Call or Premium ones are the higher-end brands.

Production: Production is a very broad term but generally means one of two different things. The first one is the equipment and staff that encompass sound, lighting, video, power, and staging. The second is an entertainment production that encompasses a group of performers that present an act or show.

Program: This word actually has three different meanings in the event world. First, it can mean the overall event or event program. Second, it could mean a specific portion of or itinerary within the overall event. Finally, it could mean the actual printed document that gives the show schedule or itinerary.

Proposal: The document you send to your client that describes the event in detail, including costs and timing. When creating this document, you should always put all of the items being proposed on hold, so that they are available and at the price quoted in the proposal. Sometimes proposals are created up to two years in advance. You are well advised to add language regarding nondisclosure and confidentiality to deter someone from copying your ideas.

Rehearsal: The practice time for entertainment, speakers, and crew to make sure all equipment, scripts, speeches, and settings are correct before the actual show or event.

Rentals: Anything that is rented for a specific time period for a specific event. This equipment can range from tables, chairs, and linens to forklifts, P&D, sound, lighting, and generators.

Rider: The part of a performer's contract that outlines specific production, equipment (backline), lodging, green room, and travel for that performer.

Riggers: The certified staff that affix the equipment to the site's ceiling.

Rigging: Suspending any item or equipment overhead in a venue. Rigging companies ensure that the points to which the equipment is being attached can structurally support the weight of the item or equipment. Rigging companies are usually contracted by the site to ensure proper suspension of equipment, proper weight loads, and the overall safety of guests by making certain nothing falls from the ceiling during the event. Venues will require you to hire their contracted rigging companies to suspend any and all equipment you may bring into the venue, even signs and banners.

Risers: Platforms used for staging. Hotels or venues use risers that are either 6'x8' or 4'x 8'. They are usually carpeted on top and have three adjustable heights: twelve, twenty-four, or thirty-two inches. Hotel risers are typically free when you contract the space. They work well for local or smaller entertainment or speakers. Larger name acts usually require bigger and taller stages, thus necessitating a call to an outside staging company.

Seating chart: The large printed document that shows table placement and identifies each table by number. Staff or guests will look at the seating chart to determine where they are supposed to be seated.

Sight lines: The view your guests will have in order to see what they are supposed to be looking at. Tall centerpieces are notorious for creating bad sight lines for viewing the stage or even across the table. Suspended décor can block or create bad sight lines for viewing video screens for presentations. Always move throughout the room and double-check for potential sight-line issues during the setup so they can be addressed before the doors open versus being helpless after the fact and having unhappy guests.

Site plan: This is a drawing of your event space with nothing on it other than the empty existing space. It gives the event space doors, dimensions, facilities, and pertinent information so that you, as the producer, can generate an accurate CAD for your event.

Skirting: The fabric that goes around the base of a banquet table or stage to hide the legs and highlight the food or beverage station. Skirting is typically pleated and attached with either pins or Velcro.

Sound and light: The equipment used for any type of production, presentation, and entertainment. This includes all lighting and audio required to produce the event.

Sound check: The time where your entertainment or band will practice prior to the event. This practice time is used to adjust all equipment levels for each band member or performer. Sound levels must be adjusted for each individual performer, such as their monitors, microphones, and main speakers. Always try to be present for the sound check so that your entertainment does not blast your guests out of their chairs. Most sound guys like it loud or are halfway deaf.

Spike mark: The little white taped "X" used to mark the floor of the stage for either a person to stand or the location for a specific piece of equipment.

Step and repeat: The printed background that is used as either a photo backdrop or for a television interview. It is usually printed with some corporate sponsor or logo. They are quick and easy to set up and provide branding opportunities for event sponsors.

Strike: The term for the takedown and removal of event equipment.

Swagging: The art of draping fabric in a stylish design. This can be done from the ceiling, stages, and walls or on tables and windows.

Table numbers: Large numbers placed in an elevated stand on the table to identify the location of each table. Guests look at the seating chart or are told their table number at check-in.

Tallboys: Forty-two-inch-tall cocktail tables, usually thirty or thirty-six inches in diameter. (See belly bars.)

Timeline: The printed document that outlines a specific part of the event. Timelines are used for event load-in and load-out, scheduling all vendors to arrive and depart at specific times. This is an essential document for a smooth, successful event and is created during the planning process. Remember: The more sweat put into the planning, the less bloodshed in the war.

Turn: Transitioning a room or space from one event to the setting for the next event. This can mean completely resetting and redecorating the entire space, such as from a meeting to a dinner or party. Smooth turns take detailed planning and precise execution from many different entities.

Underlay: The tablecloth that goes down first when using a linen combination that has a shorter overlay.

Vibe: The overall feel and mood of the event. It used to be called ambiance, but that is so eighties.

INDUSTRY WEBSITES AND JOB BOARDS

I felt it was necessary to provide a few of my industry websites that are great resources for finding equipment, suppliers, and even jobs. The Internet has been an awesome tool for the event industry, allowing buyers to find suppliers throughout the world. Good luck on your journey and next event.

www.bizbash.com

www.eventmarketer.com

www.eventpeeps.com

www.eventplannersassociation.com

www.event-solutions.com

www.ises.com

www.nace.net

www.specialevents.com

NOTES:

NOTES:

NOTES:

NOTES:

CPSIA information can be obtained at www.ICGtesting.com
Printed in the USA
BVOW020915190313

315750BV00006B/16/P